Laughing Store

Eliminate from the literature or conduct of any one people the amusing and the amused faculty, and you produce a Sterility as dull and uninteresting as the cinders and ashes of the Volcanic fields of Iceland.

(Samuel S. Cox, *in* ***WHY WE LAUGH***)

Laughing Store

A Treasury of Entertainment

Linus T. Asong

Langaa Research & Publishing CIG
Mankon, Bamenda

Publisher:

Langaa RPCIG
Langaa Research & Publishing Common Initiative Group
P.O. Box 902 Mankon
Bamenda
North West Region
Cameroon
Langaagrp@gmail.com
www.langaa-rpcig.net

Distributed outside N. America by African Books
Collective
orders@africanbookscollective.com
www.africanbookscollective.com

Distributed in N. America by Michigan State
University Press
msupress@msu.edu
www.msupress.msu.edu

ISBN: 9956-578-32-0

DISCLAIMER

The names, characters, places and incidents in this book are either the product of the author's imagination or are used fictitiously. Accordingly, any resemblance to actual persons, living or dead, events, or locales is entirely one of incredible coincidence.

Contents

Dedication

Author's Preface

I feel particularly relieved that I have finally been able to make available to the public some of those thought that make me laugh so often, even when I am alone, and which have endeared my company to so many. This, I have come to believe, is the one book I was condemned to write. When I published my first novel – *THE CROWN OF THORNS* in 1990, the 2000 copies were all sold out within a month. I learned a few weeks later, however, that many people bought or fought to buy the books mainly because they took for granted that if I had published a book then it had to be a joke book.

Although they were seriously mistaken, they, nevertheless were not totally disappointed in the novels offered entertainment of its own as well as lessons which no joke could have passed over. Life, I dare say, cannot be lived permanently on the humour lane.

A good joke is the result of the effort of the entire community in which it is produced. It is also a performance. A joke is as good as the performer. Listeners would not enjoy the joke unless you enjoy it yourself. Everybody who came into contact with me during the years in which I was gathering material for this book, has had a hand in the final production consciously or unconsciously. I am therefore referring globally to all those friends of mine, high and low, rich and poor, literate or illiterate, who worked with me every evening in the laboratories of entertainment which we call THE JEAN-PAUL CORNER in Small Mankon, Ni Richard's MIDWAY CANTEEN at Azire, Pa Allo's LOWCOST SUPPERMARKET and Pa Alfred's EXPERIMENTAL ALIMENTATION, T-JUNCTION, Commercial Avenue, Bamenda. I cannot single out any particular individuals as having contributed more. Each time I met any one of them I found my sense of humour tremendously sharpened.

I am finally indebted to the authorities of the Bamenda Hill Top Radio Station for placing at my disposal past submissions for the TCB Programme, many of which figure in here. As for the composition of the jokes printed here, originality of thought was not the issue since many of the jokes have been heard over and over before. A good joke never grows old. And much of what we consider fresh jokes are a mere recasting of old familiar ones. Come to think of it, the success of a joke invariably depends on the ability of the individual presenting it to deliver the goods.

It is not enough to announce that what you are about to say is a joke, any more than to paint the name DOG on a cat changes that animal.

Modesty, also, was not a factor of serious consideration because even the dirtiest joke will always find somebody to please. The most essential criterion for inclusion has been amusement pure and simple. And so, in my selection of these jokes, I have been extremely generous in that I have tried to provide something for everybody. Furthermore, they are fairly representative of the various categories from which most jokes can be manufactured.

As far as the categories go, they should not be taken too seriously because many would be found to overlap. My intention in breaking the material up was merely to give the reader some vague form of orientation, some mileposts to guide him in his reading or quick reference. May I take this opportunity to wish your nerves pleasant relaxation. *L.T.A*

Foreword

The intellectual world outside Cameroon knows Dr. Linus Asong mainly as the author of three extremely serious, grim but exciting novels: *The Crown of Thorns, A Legend of The Dead* and *No Way to Die*. No one laughs in these novels and only those who know Dr. Asong personally can find anything funny in those books.

In spite of the immense popularity of his novels, however, there are many, very many indeed, who would prefer a pamphlet of his humour to the ten novels, which he has threatened to publish. Here at last, therefore is his answer to that long hungry cry. As he himself said, *LAUGHING STORE* is an inexhaustible mine of entertainment for the good, the bad and the ugly.

We find here for the very first time in Cameroon literary history, in a rather distilled form, that extremely rare mental faculty of discovering, expressing or appreciating ludicrous or absurdly incongruous elements in ideas, situations, happenings or acts which John Webster and other lexicographers term humour. This is a book for all and sundry. A book for everybody who enjoys a good laugh. It is a book that will always remind you of your humanity, because philosophers have often described man as an animal that laughs! It is a book for the patients as well as the doctor; for the teacher as well as for the student; for the policeman as well as the criminal; for the warder as well as the prisoner; for the pagan as well as for the Christian; it is for the Christian as well as for the Moslem. It is for the university professor as well as the barely literate.

In a word, *LAUGHING STORE* is a book which guarantees you instant satisfaction; wherever you may be. It is the one book to take on your travels. Most important of all, Asong assures us that *LAUGHING STORE* is only the first of a five-volume series! We can hardly wait for the second volume.

Finally, and on a more serious note, Dr. Asong has revealed in his book a little bit, just a minute fraction of his bubbling self. I would not quarrel with anybody, who, after reading this book, were to conclude that humour runs in Dr. Asong's bloodstream. Or that joke gene appeared somewhere down the family tree! However, be assured that this book is not Dr. Asong's last joke!

Dr. Omer Weyi Yembe

1

FAMILY MOOBMENT

1)

"If I catch you talking to my daughter again,"
said the forbidding old man, "I kill you several times."

2)

Did you hear of the Anglophone who named
his poppy *chien*, and the francophone who named his own
dog?

3)

A visitor at a tribal meeting felt rather uneasy that he
was not making a move while everybody else invited the
President of the meeting out of a few seconds or minutes'
discussion. Not to be outdone, he finally decided to take a
chance. He walked up to the President and said:

"Let me talk to you sir."

There was a momentary look of surprise on the
President's face because he did not really know the man.
However, he went out with the visitor.

"What do you have to say?" the President asked him
outside.

The visitor hesitated for some time and then stammered:

"Nothing sir. You see, when people were calling you out
and talking to you I thought that if I did not so too, you
might think that I have something against you. That is what

1

I called you out to say."

They then returned inside the house.

4)

"And now, to end the news," the newscaster said, "here once again is the summary of the main points."

An observer asked:

"So when he summarises the main points, what will be left?"

5)

An even more daring announcer said at the end of his broadcast:

"And for those of you who will not be here tomorrow, here is tomorrow's news…" And he went on to read out fourteen messages of congratulations and two motions of support to the Head of State.

6)

As an uncle visiting from a village was eating at table he was disturbed by the presence of a little boy who just kept following every movement of his from the dish to his mouth.

"Come and take some of this *fufu* and eat," he invited the boy.

"I won't eat," said the boy.

"Then why are you just standing here looking at me like that?" the man asked.

"I want to see what my mother was telling me," said the boy.

"And what did she tell you?" the visitor asked with keen interest.

"My mother said when they give you *fufu* like this," he began, "you just cut it twice and finish it and ask for more," the boy said.

7)

Some other villager visited the same house.

The lady of the house entreated him to stay on for a meal. She prepared the food and gave to her daughter to take to the visitor.

"Only this?" the little girl asked, surprised that her mother had put such a small quantity for the stranger.

The little girl carried the food to the stranger and told him:

"My mother says this is your food, and that if you won't eat it you should give her back to eat her thing."

"I won't eat," the man said.

The girl took the food back to the woman.

Surprised she came up to the man and asked:

"I told you to wait for food, now that it is ready you refuse to eat?"

"Your daughter said you wanted it back," the visitor said.

8)

The father of a miserly gentleman died. Before dying he had asked his son to buy him a blanket. The son had done so, but had cut the blanket into two and given the man only half, keeping the other half for himself.

"Why is this blanket so small?" the old man had asked his son.

"That is how it was made," the son said. When the gentleman grew old too asked his son to get him a blanket, the boy bought one and then cut it into two and gave him only half.

"Why is this blanket so small?" the old man asked his son. The son replied:

"When grandpa asked for a blanket long ago, I saw you cutting it into two and giving him half. So I thought that is what is done when a father asks for a blanket."

9)

A mother and her little son were bathing together in a stream. The inquisitive boy looked at the naked mother and then referring to the area between her laps he asked:

"What is that?"

"It is Jerusalem," she said, trying to avoid using obscene language.

Some time later, as he was bathing with his father he asked the same question.

"Na Jesus," the man said in the same dismissive spirit. One day his elder brother who had been waiting for him to come so that they have their supper together saw him peeping through the key-hole into the room in which their parents were resting. "Na weti you de do so?" he asked the little boy.

"I de see how Jesus de enter Jerusalem," the little boy said.

10)

"I had an appointment with your husband today," the rents collector said to the half-clad beautiful wife of a tenant.

"My husband is not here. He has travelled. Come tomorrow at this same time," she said, throwing her loincloth open to readjust it. The man swallowed his spittle, took a ravishing look at the woman and said:

" Madam, minus the rentage, I can even come inside and wait."

11)

Two little boys were conversing.

"I saw my father stealing the baby's milk from my mother's breast."

"And what did your mother do? Did she not shout at him?"

"Shout? She was only laughing."

"Just like my mother too, when my father climbs on her in the night she too does not cry. But when my father says something to her in the kitchen, that is when she will begin to cry."

12)

A woman who was very suspicious of her husband's relationship with the house girl once asked her little boy to keep watch over them while she was away. On her return she invited the boy to tell her what transpired in her absence.

" Time wey you be go, papa and Esther them enter for room…"

The woman nodded, glad that she had an eye-witness account of the man 's infidelity. Instead of first listening to all of it she ran out and, calling in their neighbours and sister-in-law she urged the boy.

" So what happened?" she asked.

"Them begin for do that thing wey you de do with Uncle Ben when papa go for country."

13)

I have told you never to look a visitor in the face like that," a mother said to her son.

"I am not looking at Uncle's face," the boy said."

"I only want to see his teeth which you and papa said are very dirty and scattered."

13a)

"What do you get if you add seven francs to three francs?" the old man asked his son, hoping thereby to improve on his Arithmetic.

"The smallest franc that we have is five francs, so how can we get three francs?"

14)

"So what did you do in school today? Another concerned mother asked the son.

"Adding bananas," the boy said, and went on to illustrate:

"Our teacher said seven bananas plus nine give sixteen bananas."

"Very good," said the mother. "And if you now add seven mangoes to the sixteen bananas, what do you get?"

"We did only bananas," the boy said. "We have not started adding other fruits."

15)

A little boy who had just returned hungry from school noticed as they sat at table that the piece of meat facing his father was very big, and he wanted it.

"Father," he began, "Our Geography teacher told us that the earth rotates on its axis like this…" He swung the plate round so that the enviable piece of meat came to rest in front of him.

The father caught his game and decided to outwit him.

"Oh yes, son; "he said. "And every twenty-four hours it goes back like this…"

He had thus brought the piece of meat to where it originally belonged.

16)

A man once refused to taste his wife's food. One day he became so hungry that he decided to secretly break the vow. He entered the kitchen and took out a piece of meat from the pot of soup. He was still holding it when he heard his wife's voice. He put the piece of meat in his cap and wore it. But it was hot and the wife entered the kitchen just when it was actually burning him.

"How can you steal your own food?" the woman asked when he threw the cap down and she saw a piece of meat fall out of it.

17)

A man's quarrelsome mother-in-law had been living with them for a month. One Friday morning she announced to him;

"I am going back on Sunday, after the market day of tomorrow."

"I have heard, mama," the man said and went to work. When he returned she came up to him and repeated the announcement. This time the man did not respond. After some five minutes the woman asked:

"Am I talking to a stick?"

There was no answer.

"How can you answer a goat like me?" she asked.

The man said nothing still.

"How can you answer a goat like me?" she asked.

The man said nothing still.

"What? A goat? In my own daughter's house?" she cried, causing the daughter to come from behind the house and ask what was happening.

"Your husband says he will not talk to me because I am a goat."

"Why, mama?"

"Because I told him that tomorrow is the market day, and that I will be going back after tomorrow."

"Did I actually call you a goat, mama?"

"O.k. if you did not think that I am a goat, why did you not answer me?"

Mothers-in-law! Don't take them too lightly.

18)

The man had actually been passing to Muyuka when their vehicle broke down in Kumba. He took down the fowls, the two goats and plantains he was taking for sale in the Muyuka market and decided to spend the night with his son-in-law.

Nobody knew what had brought him there, but as soon as the son-in-law the man he received him with unusual respect because that was the first time he was bringing them gifts. The host quickly ordered the slaying of two large cocks he had in his compound. After all, he though this was a good bargain compared to what his usually tight-fisted father-in-law had brought.

They spend the whole night feasting together because I shall want to leave sharp."

"Yes, the goats and fowls. I was going to Muyuka with them to sell our vehicle broke down here yesterday. Where do you think I was carrying those things to?"

19)

As the old man went away he noticed that although his son-in-law had not mentioned it, he had expected him to leave behind the things he had brought. He decided he would make another trip to redeem his honour. He eventually made the journey, bringing two fowls, a bag of potatoes and eggs. But he was not well received. In fact, he had to go to town to buy food for himself since his daughter had travelled by the time he arrived Muyuka. When he bade the son-in-law goodbye the following morning, the man reminded him that he had forgotten his goods.

"They are for you. The first time it was for market. This time I brought these for you."

"All this?"

"All."

20)

Small Andrew thought he had really won when his father left him lying in bed and went to work. He picked up the phone and range his Headmaster:

"Mr. H.M," he began in a poorly disguised child's voice, intent on speaking the way he usually heard his father talk to the Headmaster.

"Little Andrew will not be in school today."
"Why?" the Headmaster enquired.
"He has the flu," he told the Headmaster.
"Who is speaking?" the Headmaster asked.
"My father," came the hesitant answer.

21)

The entire neighbourhood had come out to watch the Cameroonian National Football Team play its Gabonese counterparts. For 45 minutes of hair-raising suspense there were no scores. The Cameroonians, however, had hit the Gabonese goal post three times.

"This TV set is too small," said a frustrated Cameroonian fan. "If it were in the screen in my house, none of those balls would have hit the goal-post. They would have gone in straight. With this kind of mosquito screen, let them play for one year, the ball will never enter the net."

22)

It was a case of incest involving an old man and his daughter. At first he denied. But when the evidence became overwhelming against him he admitted his guilt:

"Yes I sleep with Sarah." Then as if to justify his act he asked:

"How man go cook soup i no tisam?"

23)

Pa Mati's mind was made up.
"Sustsana must leave this house," he said.
"Why?" the girl's father asked.
"She wanted to kill me," Pa Mati said.
"How?"
"She knew that the doctor had said I should not allow anything to touch my head. When we were fighting it was only my head that she was hitting. That means she wanted to kill me."

"It was a fight," the father of Sussana said.

"When you are fighting with somebody, are you the one to choose where he would strike you?"

24)

The little boy was anxious to eat groundnuts and so whenever the train stopped he would draw his father's attention to boys hawking them. The man would put him off on one pretext or another. Finally a huge man boarded the train and seemed to be coming towards where they were sitting.

"Why is that man's stomach so big, papa?" the boy asked.

"Because he eats groundnuts," the man said.

They had been going to a feast. When they got there and the food was placed on the table the guest were asked to serve themselves. The boy and his father rose at the same time that a pregnant woman too rose.

" I know what you have been doing that your belly is so big,

"the boy said aloud. "You want me to tell you? I do it sometimes too."

25)

The parents of little Tobby found it difficult to believe the story. The very delicate-looking, cowardly Tobby was said to have slapped a classmate, causing him to bleed in the nose. The class teacher confirmed the story, adding that the child had already been taken to the hospital for treatment? Tobby's parents were therefore being asked to foot the hospital bill. That evening the parents of the little victim sent in the following ill to Tobby's parents:

Worm expeller = 2,500 francs.

Ringworm ointment = 2,500 francs.

Cough mixture = 1,500 francs.

Anti-Malaria tablets = 3,500 francs.
Reader = 2,500 francs.
There is no telling what a slap on the nose can provoke.

26)

Returning from school the first day, the little boy was trashed by his father because he had lost his pencil. The following day when he returned with an exercise book missing he was beaten even more. The very next week he came home without the school bag itself.

27)

For over a month the man had been trying to teach his illiterate wife how to behave in the presence of respectable company. Once, when they sat at table with some guests, she called the house boy:

"Andrew, Andrew, bring me two spoon."

"Spoons, "the man corrected her. "Add S."

"Bring two spoon Andrew," she repeated.

"And add S."

28)

Mid-way through the dance, the old man sat restless in his chair as he watched a youth toss and swing his young wife to the rhythm of the rock music. Finally, unable to contain his uneasiness he walked up to the youth and asked:

"Why are you dancing with my wife and holding and looking only around her waist?"

"Everybody has his own style of dancing," the boy said.

"You must have a bad intention. Yours is a bad style. Anna, go back and sit down," he ordered his wife.

29)

"What right have you to harvest my fruits?" the gardener asked the young man he had caught with an apple in his hand.

"I am not harvesting it," he said.

"I saw it lying on the ground and so I am trying to return it to the tree."

30)

The man had torn his marriage certificate, which was his own way of saying he was done with his wife. He sent her back to her parents. One evening as he was entering a bar he saw the woman sitting on a man's laps and drinking from the man's laps and drinking from the man's glass.

"What are you doing here?" "Enjoying myself", she said.

"Who asked you to be enjoying yourself when the children are there suffering? Did I say you should go away and begin to enjoy yourself? Let me see you enjoying yourself again, and you will return to my house."

31)

Apparently he was just being polite when he refused to join his friends at table for lunch.

"Please, come and join us."

They tried to persuade him.

"Okay," he accepted reluctantly.

"I have already had something to eat, but let me just give you the appetite," he said and moved over to the table.

He was still licking the plates and chewing every available bone long after the others had left the table. "Do you like some more?" somebody asked him.

"Of course," he replied, having long forgotten that they had to force him to come to table.

"Only to give us appetite he ate like that, if he was really hungry…!" somebody wondered.

32)

Some would call it a case of sour grapes, but Pa Joe had much to console him when he learned that his son had not passed in a single paper in the G.C.E examination. "It is good that he has not even passed because if he passed there would be no work for him. Look at my friend Ambrose's son. Even with his degree, where is the work?"

33)

An important member of the local Council had narrowly escaped death in a major motor accident. He had then decided to offer a sacrifice in the form of a lavish party to thank God for saving his life. There was so much to eat and drink that at the climax of the ceremony the President of the tribal group to which he belonged rose to express his happiness in an emotional prayer:

"We thank you, our Father God, for this accident which you brought on our brother. We pray that You should give us many more life this."

34)

There was an old man in the neighbourhood who had lost all his children. He had come to detest the sight of children. If you passed him by without greeting, he would ask:

"How can you greet a stupid old man like me? Old age is not bought. You will one day be old, and you will see what it means for a child to pass without greeting you." If you greeted him he would say;

"Of course, why would you not greet so that I can see your white shirt? You think you are the first child I have ever seen? When you become an old man you will see what it means for a child to come and show off his new clothes before you."

35)

This reminds one of the 'Been-to' who addressed his tribal meeting in English. When he was reprimanded he reassured them:

"Even if I speak in English, I have still have respect for our culture. I know that culture is enshrined in the lives of a people…"

"What did he say?" somebody asked from the rear.

"He says he knows that culture is swine," somebody who had barely heard him answered.

"I said enshrined, I did not say swine," the young man shouted angrily.

"But between swine and shrine, what is the difference?" the President asked.

36)

In answer to request from his father for his address, the gentlemen had sent his card hopping that they would know which information was necessary. The old man got somebody in the village to write a letter for him to his son. When the letter came to the son it bore the following advertisement, or rather address:

Dr. Maximillian Essemo
B.Sc. Cotington-Liberia;
Msc. Wisconsin, Md. Padua,
Head of the University Teaching Hospital,
P.O. Box 456,
Menako,

Also
Medical Consultant of the North-West Province
Tel: (237) 36,3435-Bus;
(237) 36-6267 – Home
FAX: (663) 444-9876

37)

"Why does papa not have hair on his head?" the little boy asked.

"I think too much," the man said.

The boy turned and glanced at the wig on his mother's head and nodded several times without saying a word.

38)

A woman returned from selling garri in the market. It had rained all day, and so she had sold the garri at a heavy loss. When her daughter asked what she did with the garri that she had returned so early, she replied indignantly:

" I threw it way," meaning simply that she had sold it cheaply.

Next day they gave the girl garri to go and sell. Soon afterwards she returned.

"What happended to the garri?

"I threw it away as you did also," she said, having actually thrown it away!

39)

The woman was peeling the cocoyams and throwing into the mortar for his daughter to pound; But she did it so haphahazardly that the girl became impatient.

"Why don't you throw them on the same spot all the time?" the boy asked.

" You keep quiet and just do the pounding," she said. "Just hold the pestle ready, wherever I put the cocoyam, you pound."

By accident she threw one of the cocyams into her mouth as she waited for her to clear the heap in the mortar. The dull girl did jut what the mother said; she shattered her mother's mouth with the pestle.

40)

Here we are reminded of the blacksmith and his apprentice in Ndop Plain. The master had been trying to show the young man how and when to hit the iron so that it flattens outright.

He did it twice, but when the boy tried, his timing was poor. He would strike either too late or too early. An since they had no clock to guide them, the boy asked:

"Pa, but how do I kow when to hit it?"

"Plactice," the man told him.

"Put the iron in the fire."

The boy did.

"Wait until it turns red," he said.

The body waited.

"When you take it out," the man continued,

"look at me and wait. As soon as I nod my head, strike it at once with the hammer."

The boy did precisely as he thought his master had told him to do: He shattered his master's head.

41)

Only an intelligent parent could have detected the mischief. One of the kids was screaming and when asked why he was crying the brother said:

"He is crying because he has finished eating his sweets."

It is true that he had actually eaten his sweets.

But he had not done so at his own pace. When he threw the sweet into his mouth, the others began to tickle him, forcing him to swallow it before he had enjoyed it!

42)

The little boy was given a fifty-francs coin when the man found him weeping and turning over the dried leaves in the grass. He had just lost of fifty-francs coin which his uncle had given him for his sweets.

One hour afterwards the man saw the boy still turning over the leaves in search of the money.

"Did I not give you fifty-francs and ask you to go home? What are you still crying for?"

"If I did not lose the first fifty francs," the body sobbed, "I would have had one hundred francs now."

43)

"Why are you crying?" the lady asked the two-year old who sat lonely on the doorstep.

"All my sisters and brothers have gone for holidays…"

"But why have you not also gone on holidays?" she asked.

"I have not started going to school," the girl said.

44)

"Papa, have you come?" the little boy said to his tired father.

"Are you asking a question or greeting," the man asked.

"Greeting," the boy said

"Then say 'papa welcome', "he said. "Not, 'papa have you come?'"

45)

Pa Musali was very respectable elder of the tribe. He was struck by an illness which rendered him impotent; The relatives of his youngest wife, noticing that she was taking advantage of the man's situation to flirt around with men in the village and neighbourhood. One day relatives of the woman came to pa Musali with a suggestion which they thought could protect the man and the family from scandal.

Pa had been told of their impending visit, but not the real purpose. When they were all seated, the head of the delegation explained their purpose for coming.

"Pa, we are all one now, since you married into our family. When we heard that the doctor said your thing has died, we were very sorry. But then something began to happen; Sophie began to go about with men. That is not good for the honour of this family, and for your own self."

"So what?" the old man asked

17

"So we have come to introduce this young teacher to you. We have seen him talking with Sophie several times, and we respect him. We want that instead of allowing her to be going from one man to the other and disgracing this family, you should permit him to be helping you in…"

"Let rain water carry the roof of your houses along with you and that ya teacher and throw into the sea," Pa Musali cursed. "when a man is sick do you look for medicine or you throw him away? And who even said that my thing has died?"

46)

In order to get the job that was meant for people not less than 30 years old the young actually 21 years old man went and made a birth certificate showing that he was 35. The prospective employer looked at him for a long time, asked him a hew questions about the second World War and the Eclipse of the sun of 1945. When the boy proved totally ignorant the man said;

"Now, let us be serious. At what age were you really born?"

47)

"Say 'yes, come in' whenever somebody knocks at the door," the man was telling his wife who had just come from the village. She did very well the first day. But when she went to the toilet and somebody came and knocked on the door she said politely, and with no irony intended;

'Yes, come in."

48)

The little boy was caught stealing meat from the port of soup.

"who sent you there?" the mother shouted.

The boy tried to defend himself;

"I was just passing when my hand fell into the pot. When I wanted to remove it I saw a piece of meat hanging on it, so I jut ate it."

49)

A visitor in the neighbourhood was looking for the house of a certain Mama Matha.

"The woman red plenty?" a man stepped in to see if he could be of help.

"No," the visitor shook his head; "The woman na Bali."

50)

"When the people come in, "the man said to his little son, "tell them that I am not in the house."

He then sneaked under the bed and hid. When the tax-collectors came and enquired about him the boy said;

"He is not under the bed."

An Abreba man on his first trip to a London Restaurant saw Hot Dogs on the menu. He immediately ordered the item. Dogs, by the way, are a delicacy among the Abrebas. After a while a few sausages and some bread were brought before him.

"Where is the dog?" he enquired with great disappointment.

51)

A woman once visited her son. The wife of her son, hoping to make an impression on her decided to prepare the bet dishes for her mother-in-law. For over tow hours the young lady worked in the kitchen. Finally when the mean was set on the table and the ld woman invited to take her place, she stood at a distance, staring at the table for a very long time and then exclaimed to herself: "I never see wanda. If na so so wey you de cook for this house, how ma pikin go manage for send we money?"

19

52)

The treasurer of a tribal meeting who had ailing teeth visited his son in Britain and on his return four golden teeth had been put in the place of the bad once. It was not difficult to tell he had new teeth because in the meeting house he would laugh as if showing his teeth to a dentist, at anything you said. If you missed that he would pretend to be in pain and so as you to see if something was stuck in his teeth.

2

SOOCHOOLOO

1)
During a maths examination a beautiful girl fainted. The invigilator immediately called in the class teacher. She was rushed to the hospital in her teacher's car. Thirty minutes afterwards she was back in the room, having been told the answers to the most difficult questions.

2)
"Why do they always say Mary X-mas, and not Joseph X-mas?" asked a pupil, "when the two of them delivered Jesus on Christmas night?"

"Because Joseph had no hand in the hole thing," the teacher said.

3)
"What do the abbreviations Q.E.D. stand for?" the geometry teacher asked the class.

A small boy put up his hand and when called up, instead of saying Quod Erat demonstrandum, he said;

"Quite Easily Done."

4)
The Idioms of the English Language have to be learned. They cannot be known by sheer guess work or logic, as an exercise conducted by an English Teacher proves. During

an oral examination he chose to question the candidates on Proverbs.

"I will give the first half of a familiar proverb," he began, "and you will complete the second half."

The candidate nodded.

Teacher; "a rolling stone…"

Candidate; "Can break somebody's head. Or it can pull down a house."

5)

Teacher: A bird in hand…

Candidate; A bird in hand cannot fly away easily.

6)

Teacher; Too man cooks…

Candidate; Too man cooks work in a hotel.

7)

Teacher; Barking dogs…

Candidate; Barking dogs have every short sleep

8)

Teacher: Do not wash your dirty linens…

Candidate; Do not wash your dirty linens without omo.

9)

Teacher; Out of the frying pan…

Candidate; Out of the frying pan into the plate.

10)

Teacher; Where there is a will…

Candidate: Where there is a will somebody must have died.

11)
Teacher; Those who live in glass houses…
Candidate: Those who live in glass houses see very far.

12)
Teacher; all that glitters….
Candidate: All that glitters is usually expensive.

13)
Teacher: One man's meat…
Candidate; One man's meant cannot feed many other people.

14)
Teacher: He that is down…
Candidate; He that is down should not be disturbed.

15)
Teacher; Vox populi…
Candidate; (Instead of Vox Populi vox dei) he said Vox populi, Vox Wagon.

15a)
"No smoke without fire," the teacher said.
"What does that mean?" he asked the Form five students.
"It means that you cannot smoke unless you put fire on your cigarette," the boy said.

15b)
"Who is a monk?"
"A small monkey," came the reply.

POINT OF ORDER

Don't be too fast in dismissing the candidates because there was in most of the wrong answers a logic that made some sense. The boy who talked of Rolling Stones was no Idiot. He grew up in Sapgah, a very hilly area, and he had seen over the years the damage that stones rolling down the hills had caused to life and property.

In the same way, the boy who talked of Glass Houses knew that spectacles, sometimes mistakenly called looking glasses are often used for seeing far. If such glasses are used to build a house therefore, the occupant of such a house must be capable of seeing very far!

And then for "A Bird In Hand"! If you have caught a bird and you are holding it in your hand, the most obvious thing is that such a bird cannot fly away easily.

And, if a dog is barking, what can be more obvious than that such a dog will not sleep all night?

For "One Man's Meat…" Forget about what you know about the expression before. If meat is meant for one man, an it feed many others?

Finally, "No Smoke, no Fire."

How can you smoke without fire?

16)

A man was very anxious to see his children improve their grades ins school. One day, as an incentive, he promised to buy a bicycle for an y of the children who would come first in their final promotion examination. When they came home from receiving their report cards his eight year-old daughter ran up to him to announce;

"Papa, I took first in our class."

The excited father congratulated her and asked to see her report. When he opened it the position read 1th. Actually she had come 11th. But she needed the bicycle, so she simply rubbed off the first 1.

17)

The teacher was teaching the Prefix.

"Post," he said, "comes from Latin, meaning 'after'. For example, "Post Mortem,' means 'after death.'"

He then asked the pupils to give another example using the prefix POST.

"Post Office," one shouted.

18)

During an Algebra class in which the students had just been treating negatives and positives, a student came to the teacher and asked for permission to go out and ease himself.

"No," the teacher said.

The boy went and sat down. When he came up the second time and the man gave the same answer he walked out. On his return the teacher asked:

"when you asked for permission did I not say no?"

"You did, sir," the boy said.

"Then why did you disobey me?"

"Because you said no twice, sir," came the reply. "And you just said that two negatives make a positive."

19)

Hundreds of scientists had worked to put together the first computer. And when they felt satisfied that they had created a machine that would solve all their problems, one of them asked the computer the most baffling of all questions, the answer to which was to crown all their efforts with glory:

"How did the world start?" he asked. "See genesis," the computer said.

20)

A Prayer For Chemistry
(By Ngeh Erasmus Chanue. Sasse College, 1990)

Our atoms which act in molecules. Hallowed be thy compounds, thy mixtures come. Thy electrons be associated with protons; give us good reactions. And forgive us our unbalanced equations, as we experiment chemical hypotheses. And lead us not into forgetting atomic masses, but deliver us from careless work. For thine is the titration, alkali and acids for gas and metal; chemistry without end. Amen.

21)

A Prayer for Garri

"I believe in garri, the almighty food, maker of the tissues and the bone of all that is so delicious and lovely. I believe in garri the only son of the cassava plant. Suffered under the frying pot, was tied in mukuta bag and stored; on the third day it was brought down and pounded. He descended onto the table and waited for 1.30pm. Seated at the right hand side of groundnut and okro soup. He ascended into the stomach and was digested by the enzymes, and sent out as waste product. I believe in garri, the food almighty, the resurrector of life, the forgiveness of hunger, the satisfaction of the poor, for ever and ever, Amen."

22)

"Hip...hip...hip..." the teacher stammered.

"Hurrah!" one of the children led the cheer.

Actually he had wanted to pronounce the word hippopotamus, not to cheer up the class.

23)

Two men met in a train. As they were nearing one o the main stations one asked the other:

"E-e-e-e-e-x-x-x-c-c-u-u-u-s-s-s-e-e m-m-m-m-ee. W-w-w-w-h-h-h-a-a-t-t-t-t-t –t-t-t-i-i-i-i-m-m-m-e-e-e- h-h-h-a-a-v-v-e-e- y-y-y-o-o-u-u- g-g-g-o-o-t-t-t-?"

The man shook his head slightly, smiled gently and said nothing. The stammerer soon got off the train. As the train drove away a gentleman who had witnessed the scene said tot he man:

"You must be cruel. Why did you refused to tell the other man the time, when he took so much time to ask?"

The man began tapped his let foot five times, slapped his thighs six times and began his answer.

"l-l-l-l-l-l-a-a-a-a-a——m-m-m-mm-m-m nnnnnn-o-o-o——t-t-t-t c-c-c-c-c-rrrr-u-u-ee-l-l-l-l-l-l. l-l-l-l-l-l-l-f-f-f-f-f-f-f-l-l-l-l-l-l a-aaa-n-n-n-s-s-s-w-w——e-e-e-r-r-e-d- -h-h-e-e-e- w-o-o-o-uy-u-l-l-d-d haaaaave tttthhhought ttthat l wassss laughiiing aaattt him."

So this second man was also a stammerer!

24)

"What does it mean to say 'it rains cats and dogs?'" a teacher asked the class.

"That the rain fell on the cats and the dogs," a pupil said.

"No," the teacher said. "It just means that the rain fell heavily."

One day, after receiving a beating from the teacher the boy went up to the Headmaster and reported:

"The teacher has beaten me cats and dogs, for nothing sir."

25)

"A valley is a lowland between two hills," said the Geography teacher. "Who can give me an example of a valley?" he asked.

"The place between this girl's breasts," a naughty boy said, pointing to a girl with large breasts.

26)

"What is matter?" the chemistry teacher asked the students in a holiday class.

One of the pupils who had never had any lessons in chemistry before raised his hand. When he was called upon he said;

"Matter is when tow children are fighting or when a child is crying and the teacher asks, 'what is the matter?'"

27)

What is crop rotation?" the teacher asked the day after he had taught the children that the earth rotates on its axis once every twenty-four hours.

"Crop rotation is the movement of crops in a garden every twenty-four hours," came the answer.

28)

"It is extremely dangerous to drink tap-water directly," the school prefect said. Always remember to boil your water before drinking." One of the students who had been absent when the announcement was made that first day at school had already drunk two full cups before he learned of it. During the roll call he was absent. A quick search was conducted and he was eventually found sitting by the fire in the kitchen with his belly exposed to the flames. "What are you doing there?" the prefect asked him.

" I was not in when you said we should not drink tap water."

"So what?"

"So I made a mistake and drank it. I am sitting here so that the fire should warm it in my belly."

29)

A boy discovered that by clapping his hands in the night that prevented his friend from snoring loud. The following morning the boy said to his new room-mate;

"I could not sleep all night because you were snoring."
" I too I could not sleep," the other said,
"because you were clapping your hands."

30)

"You have all heard from the horse's own mouth," the Principal of the school said, referring to the speech the Minister of Education had just made condemning smoking and drinking amongst the students. "When I said it was an offence against the state you thought I was joking…"

"But that is no reason for you to call the Minister a horse," a policeman said. "You will have to explain."

31)

"I want you to sew another coat for me exactly like this one," a man said to the tailor. A cigarette had burnt a hole into the one he was discarding. When he came for the coat the following week, the tailor had stitched it quite all right. But since the man had insisted that the coat should be made in exactly the same way, he lit a cigarette and burned a hole through the exact spot on the new coat that it existed on the old one.

"You said I should sew it exactly the same, that I should do exactly what the tailor had done to the other one, "the tailor tried to defend himself.

32)

"Who is a mid-wife?" the teacher asked;
"when a man has three wives, " a small boy began, " the second one is the mid-wife."

33)

"Who touched this pot of soup?" a mother asked, suspicious of the fact that somebody might have tampered with the soup she had prepared for the visitors.

"I did not take any meat from inside," a small son said guiltily.

34)

The food prefect was passing near the refectory when he noticed a first year student leaning out of the kitchen window. On his own the boy came up to him and said:

"Look at my mouth, is there anything in it?"

"Why do you say so?"

"I want you to be my witness, because very soon people will say they saw me eating groundnuts in the kitchen."

35)

"What is a counterpart?" the teacher asked during a lesson in which he had just talked of the Russian counterpart of the nation's Head of State.

"The parts which the carpenter uses to make a counter," a pupil replied.

36)

"What are you drawer?" the teacher asked a pupil during the Art class.

"A cow eating grass," the boy said.

"But your book is empty," the teacher pointed out.

"Yessa, the cow has finished eating the grass and has gone him away."

37)

" A single frog is capable of laying up to two hundred eggs," the biology teacher said;

"In that case," a small boy enquired, "how many eggs will a married frog produce?"

38)

During the last minute preparations for the G.C.E the study prefect was going round when he came upon a girl sitting on a pile of books.

"What do you think you are doing?" he asked.

"Why are you not reading like the others?"

"I have tried by the head," the girl said, "but it would not enter."

39)

A teacher gave a lesson on morals and good conduct.

"If you would go to heaven," he said at the end, "you must be of excellent conduct." He spoke excitedly about the glory in heaven. Then just to find out if the pupils were listening he asked:

"How many of you are willing to go to heaven?"

Hands shot up except that of a small boy at the back of the class.

Surprised, the teacher walked up to him and asked: "You don't want to go to him and asked: "You don't want to go to heaven?"

"I want to, "he replied.

"Then why was your hand not up?"

"When I was leaving the house my father told me to come straight back to the house after school and wash my clothes before I go anywhere."

40)

"What is animal husbandry?" the teacher asked

A boy put up his hand and said:

"When you buy a female cow and then you buy a male one to live with the female cow."

41)

"What is a puppet."

"A small dog," came the reply.

42)

The history teacher was discussing the causes of the Protestant Reformation led by Luther.

"One of Martin Luther's grievances against the church was its dogmatism," he said,. Then by way of ensuring that the students were understanding him he asked:

"What is a dogma?"

"A small dog," a student said.

The teacher shook his head in denial and called on the next person. Taking his cue from the first answer he said;

"A mother dog, "he said.

43)

The college needed a science teacher. But of all those who applied for the job, the only person whose CV came close to anything scientific was a man who had done a B.A in Political Science.

The proprietor of the school invited him for an interview and there told him:

"If you can forget about the politics and teach only the science, the job is yours."

44)

It was a biology practical exam, and the children had been asked to draw the female reproductive system. Midway through the exam the invigilator received a complaint from the back of the class:

"This girl is trying to cheat, sir."

"What is she doing?" the invigilator asked.

"She is copying from the original," the boy said, pointing to a small mirror she held between her legs.

45)

"What is hollywood?" the teacher asked in a civics class.

"The wood from which they made the cross on which Jesus was nailed," came the answer.

46)

"What was the colour of the cross that Jesus carried?" the teacher asked.

"Red Cross, of course," came the answer.

47)

"Name three domestic animals," the teacher said.

A small boy stood up and said:

"Rat, cockroach and wall-gecko."

Another version has it that the child said:

"Pig, swine, kunyam."

Actually, all three mean the same thing. But when he was asked to explain the difference between the animals named he said:

"A pig is the agric kind that is white and has a short mouth. Swine is the local kind that has a long mouth and is black. Kunyam is the one that eats shit."

48)

"Abraham Lincoln was a very tall man," the history teacher began. "At the age of ten he was already five feet tall…."

"Five feet!" a student interrupted him.

"Of course," he said. "Do you think it is impossible?" he asked the student.

"I don't know sir," the little boy said. "I was only wondering how tall he was when he died."

"He died at the age of 60," the teacher continued. "Does anybody remember how tall he was when he died?"

"If he was five feet tall at the age of ten, then at the age of 60 he must have been sixty divided by ten times five…." The boy began his calculation. "Thirty feet," came the answer.

49)
"AIDS," the boy said, "simply means AMERICAN INVENTION TO DESDROY SEX."

50)
"If three men finish a job in five hours," the Arithmetic teacher began, "in how many hours will seven men finish the same piece of work if they work in turns?"

"Economic waste," the sharp pupil shouted. "If three men have already finished the job, what's the point employing seven people again? What would they be doing?"

51)
"I hear that you Africans always answer questions only with questions," the British journalist said to the Nigerian visitor.

"Who told you so?" the Nigerian asked.

52)
"Well, Mr Kojo," the Cultural Affairs Officer at the U.S. Embassy said to an African student who wanted to emigrate to America. "This English Proficiency test is your final exam. It is called the test of opposites. When I say, for example, 'black,' you must say the opposite, 'white.'"

The man adjusted his spectacles and said:

"Up."

"Down," Kojo replied.

"In."

"Out," Kojo replied.

"Together."

"Apart."

The interviewer thought Kojo knew enough to be admitted. "Very good," he complimented the candidate. But as far as Kojo was concerned, the exam was still on!

"Very bad," he said.

"No, I mean that you have done very well," the interviewer said.

"Yes, I have done very badly," Kojo went on relentlessly.

"Wait, don't understand," he cried.

"Continue, I do understand," Kojo said.

"The interview is long over," he said.

"The interview is just beginning,' Kojo said.

53)

"Dear father", the student wrote back to his father in the village after only two months in college. "I am glad to inform you that i have broken the college high jump record that has been standing for 25 years."

The message was interpreted.

"I have always known that it must be my son to do that kind of damage," he cried. "I knew that some day he will break somebody's head.

Hoe much am I going to pay for the damage?" he asked.

54)

Notice by the kitchen tap:

IT IS FORBIDDEN TO FALL DOWN WITH COLLEGE PLATES

55)

"Who discovered America in 1492?" the history teacher asked.

"I don't know sir, I was born only in 1970?"

the boy said.

56)

"The first boy in this class is a girl," the nervous teacher began to read the results.

57)

"What is the motto of this country?" the civics teacher asked.

"Peugeot 505," the pupil said.

58)

"Name three ports in the West Coast of Africa," the geography teacher said.

"Clay pot, aluminium, and iron pots, "the little girl said.

59)

It was a routine check, but there was a pleasant surprise when the external exams supervisor said:

"Candidates should place their National Identity Cards to the right of their desks as they write."

A gentleman fled through the window, even wounding himself in the process. It only went to confirm the rumour that some of the candidates who passed the exam were not those who wrote.

60)

The place was Cape Coast University in Ghana, and the occasion, the end-of-year exams. End-of-year exams in this institution were notoriously very difficult, and students had been known to lose their patience and assault invigilators when confronted with unlovable problems; Thus security guards were always posted on the alert at strategic corners, while an ambulance stood by. Invigilators were always advised to be on the lookout for any acts of disorder.

Akroma, a second year Physics students had not spent much time on his books in the course of the school year.

But when they were ordered to pen their question paper he was very happy to find the two questions they discussed the previous evening figuring on the exam sheet;

"Ha! Thank God," he shouted and threw up his pen and then caught it in excitement. According to the invigilator that was a sign of mental derangement. The man walked briskly up to the boy and seizing him by the sleeve whistled t the campus security guard to take him away.

"You think I am mad?" the boy asked, thus confirming his madness all the more. He was ejected from the exam room.

61)

Martinus had just been elected the College Senior Prefect, an honour which he meant to appreciate by doing something spectacular – he decided to produce a marathon speech of 15 pages. He wrote the speech which he read out to his classmates. They all applauded him. Then one said:

"If it were possible to reproduce such a speech by rote, it would be even more sensational." Martinus thought he could do it. An in five hours he was back amongst his mates with he result of his efforts.

Honourable prime Minister

His Lordship the Archbishop

Reverend Principal

Invited guests,

Members of staff

Fellow students,

He began, and went on to recite the speech to the end. The following day when the authorities were now gathered, he distributed copies of the speech to the guests, and then twisted his own copy and threw in the waste paper basket before the guest.

But the audience of important government authorities had quite a different impact on him than that of his classmates. And so he faulted from the first word:

Reverend prime Minister
Fellow Archbishop
Invited students…

62)

"The blazers are not enough," the principal
"We can make photocopies," a student said.

63)

The teacher wanted to know how you could eliminate
the idea of myths from a child's mind. There was, for
example, the popular belief that rain was caused when
Nganji, a certain spirit up in the sky urinated. How do you
get the child to believe that rain is caused by nimbus clouds
and not Nganji?" the instructor asked the student teacher.

"You kill Nganji, " the student said.

64)

"Who has ever heard of Côte d'Ivoire?" the man asked.
"A place where coats are made," came the answer.
"A show coat," another said.

65)

"What's a highway code?"
"The coat you wear when going on a journey," the little
boy said.

66)

"I'll see how you would eat this pie," the selfish boy said,
spitting on it to prevent his friends from begging for some.

"I'll also see how you will eat it," another said, also
spitting on the pie. "You eat my spit, I eat your spit," he
said.

67)

"Who is the most intelligent man in the world?" the teacher asked the class.

"My father," a little boy said.

"What makes you think so?" the teacher asked.

"That is what my mother says."

"And who is the most stupid person on earth?" the teacher asked.

"My mother," said the same boy.

"How do you know?"

"That is what my father says. Every evening my father says to her you are the most stupid person on earth. Then my mother says, "yes, I am the most stupid and you are the most intelligent,'" the boy explained.

68)

The biology teacher was explaining condition reflex by making reference to a banal situation.

"For example," he began, "very many years after the slave trade was abolished, at six o'clock slaves burst out crying, just because while they were still slaves their masters used to beat them every six o'clock."

69)

"Why do priests wear cassocks?" the man asked.

"So that if they see a woman they life you should not know, " came the answer.

70)

"An why do doctors wear masks when they are operating?"

"So that when you die you should not know who killed you," the small boy said.

71)

"What is the function of the head?" asked the biology teacher.

"To score corner kicks," the small boy said;

"No," another shouted. "It is to hold your hat.

72)

"What is the function of the hands?" the biology teacher asked

"To fight," the boy said.

73)

The student did not mean to be either rude or ungrateful. But what he said embarrassed the departing American Peace Corps who had been with them for five years.

"We don't want to wait until you have gone and then we begin to tell the truth behind your back," the College Prefect began his farewell speech to the American volunteer. "You were really a terrible teacher," he concluded. The woman turned red, and held her head in her hands. She felt insulted. But actually the boy meant it to be compliment. He wanted to say a "a terrific teacher."

74)

"Is it true that the higher you go the colder it becomes?" the small boy asked his two metre tall teacher.

75)

"I said 'screw driver', not "school driver"," the teacher said during the dictation exercise;

76)

"A place where you have very many plantain suckers planted in a row is called a plantation" the teacher said.

The class nodded; Then a small boy put up his hand and asked:

"But, if instead of plantains, if you plant bananas in a row; what do you all the place?"

"Bananation," another boy put in.

77)

Appointments in the Ministry of Education were said to be scandalous. It was said that they did not reflect merit. A group of townsmen sat drinking at a bar when the former principal of a High School was passing. The man's activities had so hurt the people that they had been looking for an opportunity to confront him. Insults were rained on him. Somebody said that while he was still principal he would not admit a child unless she had large breasts(in the case of girls) or the parents were extremely rich (in the case of boys).

Another customer said the man was the most inhuman creature alive because; If an old woman brought a child to him he would like to know if the woman had another daughter. Some other person said for you to get your child admitted in that school you needed to give as much as a quarter of a million francs. As they cursed and dismissed the man, a parliamentarian crept up behind them and cautioned:

If you hate the man, just keep quiet. If the government hears that he will be made a minister."

78)
(SMALL BILINGUAL SERIES)

"Chop chair" is the pidgin English word for successor. An Anglophone invited a Francophone friend to a death celebration in which the successor to a throne was to be installed. According to the tradition of the people you do not shake hands with such an authority. According to the Franco-phone upbringing, it is a sign of impoliteness to enter a gathering and down without shaking hands with he important guests. And as he carried out this formality one of the nobles invited they young an who had brought the outrageous stranger to talk to him:

"Where is your friend from? Tell him not shake hands with he chop-chair. He is just shaking hands with everybody."

The gentleman called his friend aside and tried to explain to him in French:

"Que, il ne faut pas secouer la main avec tout le monde parce que il y a des gents qui ont mange la chaise."

79)

The one shift system which was practised in the English sector of the country would have permitted the people to have the afternoons free, to work on their farms or gardens, or just enjoy themselves. Official work would then end at non on Saturdays. The government thought differently. People would work from 7.30 am to 5.30pm, instead of 8.am to 5pm. From Mondays to Fridays. They would then have their Saturdays free. The first month that this new exercise was practised the people were so happy having their weekends start from Friday afternoons that the mayor of one of the big cities phoned the Minister of Works to ask:

"This Saturday-free thing has worked so well. My people went to ask whether you think they can start working from 5.30 am to 6.30pm so from Monday to Thursday."

"And what would be the reason for that?" the Minister asked:

"So that they came have their Fridays free also."

80)

"Voilà ses fesses," the francophone boy remarked as the Anglophone girl shook her buttocks and passed by. There was an outburst of laughter.

"What are they laughing at?" the embarrassed girl asked.

"They are talking about your face," another Anglophone tried to help her out.

"Your own face, too," the girl shouted to the boy who had made the remark.

81)

The Anglophone had come to Yaounde for the first time and was amazed by the height of the buildings and the spendour of the city.

"Who get this big houses?" he stammered to a taxi driver as they drove by.

"Je ne sais pas," the taxi man said.

Further down town he saw a very long Mercedes car parked by the road.

"Who get this long motor like this?" he enquired.

"Je ne sais pas," the taxi man replied again, meaning simply that he did not know the owner.

"Jenesepas must be the richest man in this city," the stranger remarked.

82)

An Anglophone went to Yaounde and entered a bookshop to buy a diary. He did not know the French word for diary, but he knew that there were many words which sound nearly the same in French as in English. So he walked up to the hungry-looking lady at the desk and enquired"

"S'il vous plait, vous avez le diaré?"

83)

"Omam, pourqui?...Pojur Milla," the sports commentator was saying during the World Cup soccer competition. "Milla, pourqui..?

Pour Mfedge. Mfede pourqui...? Pour Nkono..."

A Nigerian trader who understood just a little French remarked:

"If Cameroon had just two other players like that Pourqui-man, they would beat any team in the world. The man is everywhere!"

83a)
"How do you say the rain is falling in French?" asked the teacher.
"Le pleuvoir tombe," came the answer.
"No," the teacher shouted.
"Le pleuvoir est tombé," the student tried to correct himself.

83b)
"Traduisez en anglais," the new French teacher said to the mainly Anglophone students, "la même chose."
"The men's shoes," came the answer.

84)
The Literature master was lecturing on the influence of the Bible on literature. He mentioned that from the beginning it was very risky business to translate the Bible into English. He went on to illustrate the point by telling the students what had happened to Coverdale, one of the early translators. He said:

"Coverdale was hunted out of Britain. He fled to Antwerp, but there his luck ran out. He was caught and deprived of the most important part of his body."

"What part was that?" a student asked. The teacher threw the question back to the class.

"What part of his body do you think he lost?" he asked.

"His penis," a bold student said.

"No," the teacher shook his head. "He lost his head. He was decapitated; Your head is the most important part of your body. There are many organs people would live without. But not the head!"

85)

A Gendarme who had been drinking in a bar rose to go to the washroom when his whistle that had been hanging from a thing rope over his shoulder dropped. An Anglophone, anxious to communicate with the Gendarme in a language he thought the man would feel better at home with, said:

"S'il vous plait, votre arbitre est tombé."

86)

This reminds me of a drawing assignment i once gave to my small boy. He was so interested in drawing football players that I asked him to draw a referee. Later on when I came into the room, I found that he had drawn a whistle and a finger pointing away from the whistle!

87)

"Who was the mother of Christ?" the priest asked the new-comer into the parish doctrine class.

"I have not even tried to know Christ himself, why should I now go on to know the mother?" the man responded.

88)

"Make a sentence with the word beans," the teacher said.

"My mother cooks beans" the first pupil said.

"I have been to church," said the second.

"we are human beans," the third said.

89)

Two men, an Anglophone and a francophone quarrelled and fought. Naturally the Anglophone gave the francophone a thorough beating; The following day when the Anglophone saw the miserable francophone passing in front of his house he thought he should call for him and apologise for what happened the day before.

"Hello!" he called

"C'est quoi?" the francophone asked.

"Please come here," I have something to tell you."

The francophone fled because he thought the man said: "Comme hier."

He would not stand another beating.

90)

"Translate into correct English," the French teacher said. "La roue de secuours."

A small boy shot up and said

"The road to school."

91)

The teacher was treating comparatives and superlatives.

"Bigger, biggest," he began, "is the comparative and superlatives of the adjective big, 'Big, bigger biggest'. Who can give me the comparative and superlative of the adjective 'small'?"

"Small, little, finish," came the answer.

3

BOY-BOY

1)

"When pronouncing such words as honourable, honest, or honour," the man told his cook, leave out the H. Do not pronounce it."

One day he left the following instructions for soup."

The cook, taking it for a test of his understanding of his master's orders he decided to decipher the real instructions. The result was: Remember to cut your air and eat the soup.

2)

The houseboy entered the room just as the lady of the house was putting on her house-coat.

"Johanes," she shouted. "Do you notice that you would have me naked in this room? "No madam," the man said politely. "I first looked through the key-hole."

3)

"When you go on jumping exercise," said the concerned mother to her daughter. "Do not jump too high because boys will see your pants."

In the evening when the little girl returned the mother wanted to know whether she was careful in her jumps.

"I jumped high, mami, but nobody could see my pants because I had removed them and hidden in the bush."

4)

He put on his underwear, and went into the bathroom to brush his teeth. He had taken out his shirt, tie and pair of trousers and placed on the bed, which he intended to wear for the day.

"Who is there?" he called through the bathroom window.

One of the servants answered.

"Before he came out of the bathroom the boy had soaked everything he had placed on the bed.

5)

"What can you cook best?" the man asked his prospective cook.

"All thing, sa, Even bread and sardine I cook."

6)

The people were talking about their servants.

"My own should be the most stupid," said one of them. "One day somebody came to the house and left the message that if I got up from sleep, he should tell me. When I woke up from sleep, he should tell me. When I woke up from sleep after three hours, this man was standing by my bed.

"What's the problem?" I asked.

"Mr. Joe said I should tell you immediately you wake up that he is waiting for your."

"You have been waiting for how long?"

"Since he went, sir. Two hours ago."

7)

A second man said:

"Just compare that with what my servant can do." He then called for his servant from behind the house and said:

"Tobias, go to the room and find out whether I am there."

"Okay sa," Tobias left. After five minutes he returned to say:

"I look everywhere sa, you no be inside there."

8)

O.K., go and dust my black shoes for me," he man said to Tobias

In five minutes Tobias was back with the shoes, filled with dust.

9)

A man once dismissed his servant who used to take care of his dog. But he soon found that he was unable to put up with the degree of thefts that were registered in his compound. The thief had no problem coming in and going away. After all, the man could not find the language in which to tell the dog that the servant had been dismissed.

10)

One day a houseboy just fresh from the village watched the Lotteries advertising with a bundle of money on TV. The following day, as soon as his master went to work the boy decided to get suddenly rich. He took a hammer and fell on the screen behind which he knew the money was hidden the previous day.

11)

"Can you make pan-cake?" the man asked his new cook.

"Pan cake is my die, sa. I can make it baad!" the cook said, implying that he could do it very well. Of course he lost the job!

12)

Before he went to bed he had told his boy that if anybody came for him he should say he had gone to town. The boy did exactly that, when a visitor came. But then, the man asked:

"When is he coming back?"

The boy ran into the room and said to his master.

"Somebody says I should ask you when you are coming from town."

13)

A certain latrine digger was arranging with a builder to provide him with material for a new latrine he had just dug for a customer. "If you give me three solid slabs 3,000 francs each.

A passer-by stepped up from behind and giving him two slaps said:

"If you give me only 1000francs for that I shall not mind."

14)

"This is 5000francs for the market," a master said to his house boy. "Buy meat, tomatoes, vegetables and all the like."

Five hours afterwards the boy showed up.

"Why did it take you so long?" the man asked.

"I buy everything sa," the boy said. "But I try and try, I no see 'all the like.'"

15)

"I have only half your salary here now," the employer told his yard-boy. "But remind me after a fortnight, and I shall clear the rest.

Exactly four nights after that the man showed up with a rope:

"This is the fourth night, sa. I have come as you said. If I don't have my money today you will bury me," he said, brandishing the rope and looking for a place to hang himself.

16)

"I am expecting a couple of visitors tonight, Ambrose," said the master. "Kill and prepared some chicken."

When the master returned that evening, all the 45 fowls in his little poultry farm had been beheaded.

"Massa been say make I kill fowl them,"

Ambrose said when asked the reason for the mass slaughter. But the trouble was not to end there because when the visitor eventually came and saw so many dead fowls in he refused to eat because he thought an epidemic had entered the farm and that his host was offering him an infested chicken.

4

USE AND SPOIL

1)

What's your name? The sports commentator asked the new player.

"Samujukuma, Kusfrabejanza."

"No," the journalist said to the coach of the team. "He will not play. Place him on the reserve."

"Why?"

"We cannot accept a player whose name we cannot pronounce in the course of the game!"

2)

"A very grateful boxer," the man said of Mohammed Ali. Actually he wanted to emphasize Ali's greatness rather than gratitude.

3)

Superstition still plays a major role in football in Africa. Teams would go all out to frustrate the efforts of the others by acquiring any juju advantage. Once upon a time, two hours before the cup final, a group of pupils ran into their coach's presence as he gave last minute instructions to the team.

"We have discovered their medicine," one of the boys announced very excitedly.

"What has happened?"

"We dug the centre of the field and discovered an egg hidden by those boys."

The news paralysed the coach because the egg had not been hidden by "those boys." It had in fact been planted by their coach himself!

4)

"This match promises to pull a record-breaking crowd," the man heard the announcer say while he was still outside the stadium. "Right now there are 5000 people watching."

Ten minutes after he entered the announcer repeated the same announcement.

"When I was outside," the spectator turned to somebody standing by him," the man said 5000. Now that I have come in, he still talking of 5000. Does it mean that I am nothing or what?"

5)

The coach's instructions were clear and unambiguous:

"But with him wherever he is. That player is always dangerous," he said, referring to the swift striker from the opposing team. Five minutes after play resumed in the second half, the coach looked in vain for his mid-fielder. finally he found him sitting by the striker on the sideline. The striker had been replaced but the boy had learned always to obey his coach.

6)

At an inter-village soccer match, a disputed penalty kick occurred. The chief of the village of the victimized side ordered his servants to carry away the goal posts to his place.

"If they want to score let them come and score in the palace," the chief said in throttled anger, leading both his team and the goat-posts away. The match was cancelled.

6a)

Another version has it that as the chief and the goal posts were arriving the palace they heard a loud noise from the direction of the playground. He sent a servant to go and find out the reason for the noise.

"Mbe," the servant began on his return, "the referee asked the goal keeper to go to the other goal post and catch the penalty."

"And what happened?" the furious chief enquired.

"They kicked and scored, Mbe," came the answer.

7)

"I don't like the look of this team," the newly elected patron of the club pointed out. He then gave the captain 50,000francs, saying:

"Use this to lift this club to championship calibre."

The team which had not won all season, won the next two matches, but the patron was not impressed because the team still dressed very shabbily.

"I gave you money to help this team look respectable," he said to the captain.

"Yes, sir."

"But what happened?"

"We divided the money into two, sir. We gave 25,000francs to the referee of the first match, and 25,000francs to the referee of the other match."

8)

"Penalty," the referee blew his whistle and shouted, pointing to the penalty spot. The ball was placed. The man to take the kick was some two metres tall and weighed about 120 kilograms. He walked some fifty metres from the ball and then began charging.

The referee blew his whistle to halt him.

"What is happening?" the player asked furiously.

"Then is no goalie," the referee pointed out.

Then he went up to the goalie standing away from his net and asked:

"Any problem?"

"If you won't choose another player to kick that penalty, take it as a goal. That man can kill somebody. See how big he is, and see how far he started running from, only to kick that small penalty!"

9)

It happened at the Bamenda Tennis Circuit.

The home doubles team had taken the first set 6-0 and was leading the Yaounde squad 3-0 in the second set. Thus the scoreboard read

BAMENDA-1,

YAOUNDE-0

An excited Bamenda fan looked up at the scores and asked:

"How did Yaounde even get the zero? Don't give them anything."

10)

during an inter quarter football match a penalty kick was awarded to one of the teams.

The player taking the kick tricked the goalie so that he went up when, in fact, he shot low.

The ball did not go straight into the net but hit the goalie flush on his genitals.

Two minutes afterwards the man who had just kicked the ball saw a woman chasing him out of the field with a stick. When she was caught and questioned, she asked:

"Another place no be dey wey yi be fit shoot ma man?"

11)

Two tennis matches were taking place at the same time on two adjacent courts. A gentleman standing on the fence that separated the two courts placed a piece of cardboard vertically along the line of his nose and between his two eyes.

"What are you doing?" somebody asked him.

"I want to see both matches at the same time.

I want the left eye to see the match on the left court and the right eye to see the match on the right court."

12)

The Mezam Division was hosting the last match of the First Division soccer season. A Peace Corps Volunteer, apparently disgusted with the tempo of the match asked a spectator:

"Which Division is this one?"

"Mezam Division," the spectator said, thinking that the man wanted to know the name of the division in which the match was being played.

"No, I mean the division of the teams," the white man tried to make things clearer.

"The one in green is from Menchum," the spectator specified. "And the one in yellow is from Mezam here."

13)

Following the marvellous performance of the Cameroonian National Soccer Team at the 1990 World Cup, the Columbia coach asked his Cameroonian counterpart:

"If your lions are that Indomitable, how come they got whipped 4 zip by the Russians?"

He was referring to the beating the Cameroonians had just received from the Russian team for whom the victory was meaningless anyway, since they were out of the competition.

"No real Lion eats dead meat," the Cameroonian coach said.

14)

The local team had virtually clinched their place into the finals of the soccer competition with their one goal lead when with only two minutes left the striker of the visiting team kicked the goalie and fell into the net. The irate goalie charged into the net to take his revenge. The referee's whistle went.

"Goal," the referee said, pointing to the centre.

"But I caught the ball," the goalie said.

"Then why did you cross the goal line with it?" the referee asked.

"I just wanted to kick him back," the goalie said. "He kicked me."

The referee's decision stood. The game was now tied at one goal each.

15)

With Forty-five seconds left, the goalie caught the ball again, only to be kicked once more by the notorious striker of the visitors. The goalie was furious and wanted to revenge at once.

But he wanted to be wise.

"Just hold this ball for me," he said, giving the ball to his defenceman. "I wan to teach that idiot a lesson he will never forget."

The rules are clear on this. Anybody else touching the ball within the penalty circle who is not the goalie commits a grievous offence.

"Penalty," the referee blew his whistle.

The local side lost by a score of one goal to two, with just enough time left to centre the ball!

16)

He was wearing a crash helmet, bullet-proof jacket, front and back, shinguards, goggles, boxing gloves, two pen knives dangling from his belt and a pistole stuck to his side.

And who do you think he was?

A first division soccer referee in Gabon.

Gabonese fans had been notorious for molesting referees.

5

WASPITA

1)

No such thing had ever been heard or seen in the neighbourhood:

"A baby has just been born with four teeth in its mouth," the midwife was telling a nurse.

"Find out about the father," the listener said.

"He must be a dentist."

2)

a couple once went to a medicineman to whom it paid 10,000francs for the services to be obtained: they had come to ask for the son to be cured of Kleptomania and blatant lie telling. And the man had promised to get rid of both.

"as we are all sitting here," the medicineman told them, "for any lie that anybody tells, he will receive a knock from the stick. "He pointed a baton that suspended from an almost invisible string over their heads. "So tell your story," the medicineman said.

"We don't know what to do with this boy," the mother began. "Everyday reports must come to us that he has stolen something."

"Is he following the footsteps of any of you?" the medicineman asked.

"No!" the parents refused.

The baton struck first the woman and then the man.

"Are you fund of telling lies?" the medicinman asked the man.

"No," he said, receiving a knock at the same time. Then the stick did one strange thing, it swung over and struck the woman without her saying anything.

"Have you ever brought a woman to your house in your wife's absence?" the medicineman asked the man.

"Never."

Two knocks.

"Have you ever brought a man into your bedroom in your husband's absence?" the medicineman asked the woman.

"I have never."

Three knocks.

"And you think the boy invented the will to steal? Get out of here!"

3)

"Why not try some other cure, doctor?" the nervous patient asked. "I cannot stand an operation."

"I know exactly how you feel," the doctor said.

"Sure doctor, have you ever been operated upon before?"

"No," the doctor denied.

"Then how do you know how I feel?"

"Because this is also my first operation."

4)

A hormone for intensifying sexual activity in men was invented at the Ibadan University Teaching Hospital. It needed to be tested on a familiar animal, but one whose sexual activities are least obvious to man.

The vote fell on the cat; No sooner had the female nurse administering the injection withdrawn the needle than the cat jumped from the table; Knowing the purpose of the experiment, the first thing the woman did was to immediately clasp hr apron tight between her legs.

The possessed cat jumped over the hospital fence into a poultry far; Two hundred and fifty eggs later hatched kittens.

5)

The recovering patient had vacated his bed to make room for a more serious case in the accident ward. A new nurse had just taken over duty when the relatives of the patient came in to enquire about their brother.

"Think he died," she said; "Ask from the mortuary," the nurse added.

"Are you the one who carried me to the mortuary?" the patient asked from the bed in the next compartment. "If you are not careful your mouth will be the first to carry you there."

6)

A certain native doctor who was said to be capable of curing insanity had a peculiar way of diagnosing the gravity of the cases brought to him. Without asking any questions he would order his boys to fall on the patient and beat him hard with sticks. If the patient cried and ran away, he knew the case was within his reach to cure; But if he just stood there staring at him, he refused to meddle with him. His medicines must have worked very well because he enjoyed an enormous popularity. One day a man jumped down from a bus that came to stand near the doctor's house and ran towards him. He was really coming to tell him that he had a patient in the bus and needed some help to get him out. The medicineman mistook the visitor for a patient and immediately ordered his boys to ascertain the degree of his own madness.

7)

Alhadji Baba was seriously sick, so his children rushed him t the General Hospital. The doctor on duty examined him carefully and declared that the case required a surgical operation.

The theatre was set and Bana was soon placed on the operating table. Then all of a sudden, Baba dipped his hand into his inner pocket, brought out a bundle of money and started counting the notes aloud.

"You don't have to pay until after the operation," said the doctor.

"what said I was paying?" Baba asked. "I want to know how much money there is in my pocket before you give me that your injection.

I don't want to get up and not know how much has been stolen."

8)

A pretty young woman with a baby came to see the doctor. She was shown into the hospital's examination room. The doctor examined the baby, and then asked the woman:

"Is he breast-fed or bottle-fed?"

"Breast-fed," she answered.

"Strip to your waist," the doctor ordered her.

She did and he examined her. He fingered her breasts. Then, he squeezed and pulled them, and sucked on each nipple. Suddenly he remarked:

"No wonder this child is suffering from malnutrition. You, his mother don't have any milk in your breast!"

"That's right," she replied. "He's my senior sister's child, not mine."

"I don't know," said the doctor. "Then you shouldn't have come."

"I didn't come till you started sucking on the second one… " she said panting.

9)

"Phensic," the pharmacist said with infinite patience to the village, "does not cure fainting sickness."

"Then why them call'am feint-sick?" the man asked.

10)

"Do you sometimes hear noises, several different noises, without knowing who is making them?" the psychiatrist asked the patient.

"Yes, sometimes," the man replied.

"On what occasions?" the doctor asked.

"In the market place," he said.

11)

Still at the psychiatrist, the patient told the doctor;

"I cannot tell what is wrong with me. I seem to forget nearly everything. Even the colour of my car, my wife's name, sometimes, even my house."

The doctor nodded for a long time, took down some notes and then asked him:

"For how long have you noticed that this is happening to you?"

"You mean this what?" the patient enquired.

He had already forgotten what he was telling the doctor.

12)

"Have you been taking the medicines I prescribed for you?" the doctor asked his patient whose case did not seem to improve.

"No, doctor," the old woman said.

"And why did you not take it?"

"I did not want to disobey the instructions," the woman said, pointing to the label on the bottle: KEEP BOTTLE TIGHTLY CORKED ALWAYS.

13)

A woman entered a doctor's office and sat staring at him without saying a word.

"What is your problem?" the doctor asked finally.

"Pimples, doctor, I used to have only a few.

Now they are all over my body."

"No need to worry, madam,' the doctor said.

"They are just having a general session."

14)

Th disease cannot just be controlled, it can be cured completely," the man told the family of the epileptic child. "I have a very good friend of mine who had it for several years…"

"and now he no longer has it?" the mother of the child enquired with great interest.

"Completely gone; I will ask him how he did it and then get back to you."

The following day he went up to his old friend and drawing him aside said:

"There is a family friend of ours whose daughter has epilepsy. What did you use to cure yours?"

"Who told you that I had epilepsy?" the man asked. "Convulsion and epilepsy, are they the same thing, If your business is to go about spoiling people's names, leave my name out."

15)

The nurse was returning from the lab with a urine specimen to be used as part of her qualifying exam when the test-tube fell and broke. Afraid to face the ire of the doctor and so betray herself as undeserving of the certificate she dashed into the nearby toilet and filled another test-tube with her own urine.

After careful analysis the doctor called the gentleman whose rune was supposed to have been analysed and told him:

"You have just made medical history?"

"How, doctor?"

"You are three months pregnant."

16)

"I think you have gout," the doctor told the man.

"What is gout, doctor?"

"A form of arthritis that results from eating meat…"

"What kind of meat?"

"Cow meat."

"It can't be, doctor."

"What makes you think so?" the doctor asked.

"Do cows have gout?"

"They don't," the doctor told him.

"if the cow itself that carries the meat about does not have that your thing you call gout, how can i have it just by eating a small fraction of that meat?"

"Perhaps if the meat that the cows carry about were cooked meat," said the doctor, " they too would have the gout."

17)

The native doctor looked serious about curing the woman of her sterility. But the husband did not like his approach. The native doctor had told the man:

"Just give me this woman, I work'am for three months, if i no get twins, know say I be nonsenseman."

"So you go d how?" the worried husband asked.

"Just leave'am for me. I go do the thing wey you never do for the woman."

The man chose to live with the sterility instead.

18)

The king had developed an abscess between the legs. A nurse was asked to prepare the infection for a surgical operation. The king pulled down his pants, the woman took one look at him and said to herself:

"God save the queen!"

19)

"You need antibiotics," the pharmacist said to the young man.

"I have tried all sorts of antibiotics," the boy said.

"Then try uncle-biotic," the boy said.

"Then try uncle-biotic now," some passer-by said.

20)

An old woman came to the General hospital to visit her son. As she approached the glass door into hers son's ward, she mistook her reflection for somebody barring her way.

"Please, I am just begging you to allow me to go in and see my son," she pleaded. Just then, a nurse who had heard her begging opened the door and asked her to go in.

According to her, politeness had paid off.

21)

"Do you drink beer?" the doctor asked the man who had reported with a case of trembling hands.

"I cannot hide anything from you doctor, I drink beer, doctor," the man confessed.

"About how many bottles a day?"

"If I buy myself, doctor, I an drink like three bottles."

"But if somebody buys for you, how many can you drink?"

"What? That one, doctor! Until the man stop for buy I cannot fit stop for drink. Or until the beer finish for bar."

22)

The police, not very much in anybody's good books these days, arrived the scene of a fatal accident within minutes of its occurrence and quickly set to work to recover the bodies in the shattered vehicle. Some eight passengers were already dead, one of them, a policeman lay with his head completely severed. One of the very lucky few with his foot trapped between the iron bars of the twisted seats was creaming for help and pulling at the officers as they forced their way into the vehicle.

"You just shut up your dirty mouth," the officer shouted at the screaming passenger.

"Whom do you thing you are? Look at a whole policeman lying there with his head cut off, he is not even saying anything. And you with only a wounded toe you won't allow somebody to pass!"

23)

All the passengers involved in an accident had been declared dead by the authorities who were called to examine them. Accordingly, their pockets were searched for identification papers which were taken to the Radio Station. There an announcement was made calling on the friends and relatives of the identified persons to report to the Mortuary of the Provincial Hospital to take away their remains.

A family showed up late that night and insisted on taking away their deceased brother. It would appear that the announcement that all the passengers had died was not quite accurate.

At least one person had been declared dead and thrown into the mortuary when he was merely unconscious. The man regained consciousness after sometime and started feeling his way round the dark room, his pocket radio singing.

He did not know where he was; In fact, he even thought that he was in his house. So when he heard people trying to open the door he quickly enquired from within:

"Who is that? Please wait for me to light the lamp."

Who would wait for a corpse to light a lamp in the mortuary? The people ran for their lives.

24)

"Do you have medicine for modern maths," the student asked the medicineman for a solution to a thorny problem in his academic programme;

The medicineman had claimed that he had medicine to solve all problems.

The man nodded several times and then told the boy:

"You are lucky that you have come straight to the right man because that thing you call…"

The boy repeated the name.

"Yes," the man resumed," that thing killed very many people before they knew that I have the medicine for it."

25)

The popular radio announcer showed up at the maternity word to send home to loved ones messages of births.

"So, madam," he began in his usual friendly tone, "what news do you want to send back home to your people about this very beautiful baby girl that you have delivered?"

The woman sobbed three times and then began stammering;

"They should tell my husband not to blame me that I have delivered a girl again… They should tell him that <i tried and tried, and tried, but only a girl came out…"

"But why should anybody blame you? Your husband should be happy instead for such a nice-looking baby girl," the announcer tried in vain to soothe her.

"They should beg him because he said before I left the house that if I did not deliver a boy I should not come back to his house any more."

"How man children do you have, madam?" the announcer asked.

"Ten," she said.

"Ten," she said.

"How many girls?"

"Ten," she said, bursting into tears.

26)

A neighbour came to visit Mrs Ngum who delivered some days before.

"Sister, na why you still be here till now? The child de sick?" she asked.

"No, "Mrs. Ngum said. "You know when you deliver man pikin so, doctor get for castrate'am first before you go house."

"So the doctor dong make'am?"

"Yest," she said. "We de leave tomorrow."

27)

This reminds me of an incident in which a man brought his dog to the veterinary. There he told the official on duty;

"I want make them circumcise my dog."

It is interesting how many people still confuse castration with circumcision!

28)

"Do you have any allergies?" the doctor asked the woman as he fingered his pencilling injection..

"Legies, legies, legies," the woman repeated to herself, reflected and then said;

"I no get, doctor, but I can ask my husband to buy some when he comes here."

29)

"I was driving, not really too fast," the man was describing an accident in which he was involved. The suddenly from the middle of the road I only saw myself in a house with half the car inside..."

"Then it is not your fault," said a sympathetic relative. "What was the house even doing in the middle of the road?"

30)

An empty coffin was being transported in the open back of a pic-up truck to the hospital to bring home a corpse. A stranded traveller stopped the vehicle and asked for a ride in the direction of the hospital.

"If you can manage behind with the coffin," the driver said. "There is no more room here, as you can see."

The man jumped to the back very gratefully and they drove on. When it suddenly began to rain the traveller decided that since the coffin was empty he could as well enter and protect himself from the heavy rain.

Two more people stopped the kind driver and asked for a ride as the rain was becoming very heavy.

"If only you won't mind sitting behind with an empty coffin," the man said. The rain eventually ceased and, tired of standing up the two men decided to sit down on the coffin. One of the men said he thought he heard a sound inside the coffin.

"It can't be," the other said. "Did the driver not say the coffin was empty?"

"Don't let me die inside here," a strangled voice said from inside; "Who said it was empty?"

The two men jumped from the speeding vehicle, wounding themselves, as the lid of the coffin was thrown open and a man emerged from within.

31)

Three patients were hauled before the judge for beating up a third patient in the hospital. Both men pleaded guilty, but why it ever happened was of interest to the court. The victimised patient had been told in the village that in the hospital the doctors took care only of the very serious cases, that o be treated he needed to make his case really serious. Thus, each time a doctor was passing to visit the sick in the nearby ward, the man would scream, fall from his bed and

roll. This would attract the attention of the doctor who would come over to him and discuss his problem and prescribe drugs. As a doctor was passing in front of the ward the man started screaming again; Two patients in the neighbouring ward who had discovered the man's trick fell on him and beat him up, saying:

"If you think you are more sick than any of us, you will show us now."

32)

"Always shake the bottle before drinking this medicine," the doctor told the patient. The forgetful patient accepted, but before he remembered the instructions in the evening he had already swallowed the two spoons that were recommended. As the doctor was making his rounds he heard a man jumping continuously from the patient's ward. He came up to him and asked.

"Why are you jumping and disturbing the rest of the patients?"

"Doctor," the man began, "I forgot to shake the bottle of medicine as you said, before drinking. I am trying to make it mix up in my stomach."

33)

The Cup Final was to take place in mid-August, and the one thing people dreaded mot was rain.

"I know a rain-maker," somebody said. "If you give me 10,000 francs to take to him, he will hold back the rain until after the match." The match-delegate gave him the money and they set out with two scouts to meet the rain-maker. When they arrived a sport at the end of the village where the man had claimed the rain-maker lived, he saw no house.

"There used to be a house here, not so?" he asked a neighbour.

"Yes," the man said.

"What happened to it? We are looking for the rain-maker who used to live here."

"Aaah, that man, na tiefman. Water rain be dong carry yi and the house go withéam."

34)

Another man put out a reward of 5,000 francs for anybody who would lead him to the greatest witch-doctor. A young man led him to Cameroon Wonder, the quintessential medicineman.

"I want you to install medicines on my plantain farms, such that if a man attempted to steal anything, he would remain standing there until I came and caught him."

"Easy thing for me," Cameroon Wonder said. He demanded a fee of 50,000 francs which was promptly paid. The two men drove to Batibo, some 200, kilometres away to install the medicines.

But both the money and the trip were wasted because while they slept in the night in Batibo to install the medicines the following day, thieves raided their house and stole the entire box of medicines.

35)

After seven years in the Second Division the coach decided that he must use other means to climb to the First Division of the national soccer competition. He decided to visit a medicineman.

"I am even surprised that it even took you so long to come and ask for my help," the medicineman said. "All the teams in the First Division know me very well."

He promised to put the team in the First Division on two conditions:

First, a fee of 300,000 francs. When that was paid he asked for the bleeding claw of a wild cat.

After two week the coach showed up blind in one eye and scratch-wounds all over his face.

"I think it will be better for the team to remain in the Second Division with my body intact than go into the First Division with me blind," the man said, demanding the refund of his money.

"You cannot go from Second to First Division like that," the man said, "without losing something."

36)

The nurse was explaining in the most modest terms, how to use condoms as contraceptives;

"Before you do it," she began, "you just take the thing and slip it in like this. " She held up her forefinger and slipped the piece of rubber tubing over it. "And then you go ahead and do your thing," she went on. "After that you fell it to make sure that there was no leakage. You take it off, and that's it."

The woman who had come to learn how she could stop having children without sacrificing her sex life returned home and explained to her husband exactly what she had been told. Two months later she came to the clinic and reported. She was pregnant.

"Did your husband use condoms?

She agreed.

"Did you detect anything unusual at the end of the exercise, say a leak and the like?"

"Nothing."

The nurse explained again, in very modest terms, holding up one finger, slipping in the condom and then removing it again after the exercise. But when the woman reported with a cause of pregnancy the next time the nurse asked her to demonstrate precisely how her husband did it that it produced such poor results.

"I would climb on the bed," she said. "I would lie down like this, then my husband will hold his finger in the air as you did, and slip in the condom as you said. Then he will go ahead. When he has finished he would put his finger down and…"

"You mean your husband wears it on his finger instead?"

"Yes, was it not what you…"

"That was just a demonstration. I thought you would understand what I meant if held up my finger."

37)

"How are you?" the doctor said to the patient.

"Fine, doctor."

Fine then why you come here?"

"I think say doctor be just de greet me."

38)

Four men sat on a bench outside a maternity waiting for news about their wives who were in labour; After some two hours of waiting a nurse came out and asked;

Who of you is Mr. Bonkiyung?"

The man rose.

"Congratulations, your wife has just had a bouncing baby boy."

Just then one of the people rose in protest:

"You will never stop cheating in this hospital.

My wife came here first, and I came before this man."

39)

A man who had heard very many scandalous tales about the activities of doctors with women patients in their offices brought his wife to see the doctor. The doctor took the woman in to an adjoining room to examine her. He then placed the woman on a bed. Spying from under their door blind the man noticed that here were only two legs standing instead of four. Let the two remaining legs disappear too, he told himself, and I will tie the of them on that bed; When he next looked, true to his fears, there were no more legs on the floor. Grabbing a bottle he charged into the room only find the doctor returning from an inner office where he had gone to take an exercise book in which to note his diagnosis!

40)

A nurse was passing through a playground one evening when he noticed some boys using the blade to make marks on their arms.

"You don't know that AIDS can be transmitted when one person's blood comes into contact with that of another?" she asked.

"No way, one of the boys said, and then went on to prove his point. He squeezed another from his wound, mixed the two on his palm and the holding the palm to the nurse asked:

"Okay, where is the AIDS?"

"I don't mean mixing it that way," the nurse went on, determined to convince them. "When the blade that has just wounded you touches your friend's wound, he can have AIDS."

"It cannot," the boy said.

"Why not?" she asked

"Because we are wearing condoms."

41)

The wife of the first son of a certain family was said to have given birth to a handicapped child. When the parents of the child visited the new-born in the hospital the father-in-law of the woman who had just given birth looked at the baby with only one finger sticking out of the stump of his hand and cried: "With only one finger, how will he ever be able to slap his wife and she will feel it?"

42)

A man whose wife was expecting their 9th child was waiting on a bench outside the delivery room with a bar of soap and a slam towel when the nurse came and announced:

"Pa, congratulations, you dong get boy pikin."

The man jumped for joy because the eight other children were all girls. As he was walking way the nurse came out again and, calling after him told him:

"Pa, congratulations again. Madam dong born another pikin!"

"Eh-eh!" the man wondered. "Now now so, nine months dong just reach!"

"No, pa, na twins."

The man walked back disappointed. He now had to prepare to take care of two children instead of one. While he sat on the bench pondering the doctor came out himself and announced:

"Pa, actually, na triplets wey your woman get. I dey like say another pikin still dey for yi belle."

"Doctor," the man began "na bad play that.

"You no fit tel yi make I stop'am so? Pikin dem de comot you de lefam so say na who go main'am?"

6

PORITIC, PORISS AND THE DAW

COMMUNICATION (COURTESY OF READER'S DIGEST)

A)
A COLONEL ISSUED THE FOLLOWING DIRECTIVES TO HIS EXECUTIVE OFFICER:

"Tomorrow evening at 20,00 hours Harley's Comet will be visible in this area, an event which occurs only once every 75 years. Have the men fall out in fatigues, and I will explain this rare phenomenon to them. In case of rain, we will not be able to see anything, so assemble the men in the theatre and I will show them the films of it."

B)
EXECUTIVE OFFICER TO COMPANY COMMANDER:

By order of the colonel, tomorrow at 20,00 hours, Harley's Comet will appear above the battalion area. If it rains, fall the men out in fatigues, then march them to the theatre where the rare phenomenon will take place, something which occurs once every 75 years."

C)
COMPANY COMMANDER TO LIEUTENANT:

"By order of the Colonel in fatigues at 20,00 hours tomorrow evening, the phenomenal Harley's Comet will appear in the theatre. In case of rain, in the battalion area, the Colonel will give another order, something which occurs only once every 75 years."

D)
LIEUTENANT TO SERGEANT:

"Tomorrow at 20,00 hours, the Colonel will appear in the theatre with Harley's Comet, something which happens only once every 75 years. If it rains, the Colonel will order the Comet into the battalion area."

E)
SERGEANT TO SQUAD:

"When it rains tomorrow at 20,00 hours the phenomenal 75 years old General Harley, accompanies by the Colonel will drive his Comet through the battalion area theatre in fatigues."

1)

"That the butcher raped you?"

"Yes," the woman said to the lawyer. The husband had planned to make a case of it.

"Where was that?"

"In the market, behind the stall," she said.

"And did you shout?"

"In the market, behind the stall," she said.

"And did you shout?"

"No"

"Why?" the lawyer asked.

"He promised to give me three free kilos of meat."

2)

"On what grounds did you insult his wife" the lawyer asked the impudent man who had been hauled to court for persistently making derogatory remarks against his neighbour's wife.

"It was not on the ground, your worship," the man tried to defend himself. "It was on the veranda."

3)

"Do you know that money-doubling is an offence against the state?" the judge asked the accused.

"I do, your worship."

"Then why did you involve yourself in such a nefarious act?"

"Your worship," the man began most politely,

"the head of state was always complaining that there was no money in the country, so I thought I could help the country if I…" "Shut up!" the judge shouted. He got ten years.

4)

"Did you raise an alarm?" the policeman asked the suspect.

"I could not, sir."

"Why could you not?"

"There was no lamp."

5)

"What do you do for a living?" the judge asked the young man who was being accused or robbing a store.

"Small bisnet, ya worship," the boy said.

"What kind of small business? Tell the court precisely," the judge insisted.

"I sell second hand things," the boy said.

"That is still not precise enough. Second hand things like what?"

"Like toothbrush, toilet roll, handkerchiefs, ladies pants…"

"I beg, that's enough," the Judge pleaded. As a matter of fact, in the boy's mind, retailed articles were the same as second hand.

6)

"If it is a lie, Your worship," the accused swore, "let a volcano enter this court and carry me away…"

"Enter whose court?" the judge asked. "Say the volcano should enter your house. Are you the only person in this court?"

7)

"Why did you slap the nurse?" the judge asked the patient.

"She came and was disturbing me," the man said. "She knew that i had not been sleeping for several nights, and just when i felt sleepy she came and woke me up."

"And why did you disturb his sleep?" the judge asked the nurse.

"I wanted him to woke up and take his sleeping pills, your worship."

"But if he was already sleeping," the judge said, " that was good reason to leave him alone."

"The doctor said I should always give him before he went to bed, your worship."

8)

"Two years or five hundred thousand francs?" the judge asked the condemned criminal.

"Let me take the money, your worship."

9)

"Where are you going to?" the bus driver asked the man standing by three bunches of plantains.

"Tiko." The man said. "How much will I pay?"

"One thasen francs," the driver said.

"How much for my plantains?"

"No charge," the driver said.

"Then you take my plantains. Na because of the plantains I be want take bus, the man said.

"I shall walk there."

10)

"Mr. Amabo", the Jude bellowed, "you are charged for owing your landlord ten months rents, threatening him with a cutlass and calling him a rogue. Guilty or not guilty?" The man looked defiantly at the judge and said:

"Not guilty, ya worship. I owe only nine months rents, not ten months. I did not call him a rogue. I called him a thief. And I did not threaten him with a cutlass. It was a small knife."

11)

The woman was appearing in court for the first time as witness to a fight in which somebody had died. She had been told by friends that there was a group of people in court called *lawyers* who could derail and even implicate an innocent person. She was therefore bent on telling it as she saw it, all of it.

"No," the lawyer told her. "Just answer yes or no."

She would not. She was determined to retell the whole story after every question. The judge banged his desk impatiently on the dais above them.

"Madam, don't waste the court's time, please answer a simple yes, or no."

She looked up and seeing the judge for the first time did not know that he had anything to do with what was happening between her and the lawyer.

"na who too be that one for dey so? As we de talk here, na who dong ask you question? Why you dey enter for tin wey i no look you?

12)

The man had been involved n a fight in which a neighbour had lost his life; his lawyer had warned him not to admit that they fought. He should say he was attacked and he tried to defend himself. But somehow, when they were all assembled in court the lawyer's advice slipped from the accused's mind. Thus, when the judge asked:

"So na you beat that man kill'am?" the man answered.

"Yes, we be fight. But I get my lawyer here," he said pointing to his lawyer. The man turned his face away.

13)

The man had been locked up for stealing a goat. A lawyer had been hired for 75,000 francs, but he could only pay 50,000 francs at the time

"You pay the rest after the judgement, then?" the lawyer asked.

The man agreed. In court the young lawyer defended the thief so well that he was acquitted and discharged; A few hours afterwards the lawyer was at his door to claim the rest of his money.

"Balance for which case?" the man asked the lawyer.

"The case for which you nearly went to prison."

The man grinned for some time.

"M"? Steal goat?" he asked. "Are you not the same man who was swearing the bible in court that I am not the kind of man to steal? I don't believe any more that I could have stolen the goat. In fact, I was even wondering how I would get the rest of the money from you."

14)

The housemaid took her master to court for dismissing her. The main reason for the dismissal was her persistent refusal to go to bed with him. By way of assembling the necessary information the lawyer asked the woman:

"For how long have you worked under this man, madam?"

The woman stood apparently scandalized for whole minute and then she said:

"No one day, sa. Everyday mater de ask me I de refuse, i ask me i refuse. I say i be married man, I no fit gree for work under yi."

84

Apparently, to her, working under somebody meant lying down for slpething to be done on her!

15)

A man was summoned to appear in court for provoking a fight during a boundary dispute with a neighbour whose son was named Innocent. As the charges were being read against him he pleaded.

"I am innocent, your worship…"

The neighbour jumped from his seat and shouted:

"Even that one, ya worship, is lies. I know his name. Innocent na the name of my son. Not his name."

16)

The evidence against the man was overwhelming. He had been found near the bank, late at night, with a hammer, a dagger and a sack.

"Loitering with an intent to rob the bank," the judge said.

"That is not enough to convict me, your worship," he said. "Just because i was carrying all that doesn't make me guilty. You could as well arrest me for rape since I am carrying with me here, the necessary equipment for rape."

17)

"What exactly is the charge?" the judge asked the chief of security who had caused a man to be brought to court, be tried and then jailed at once.

"I overhead this man asking an Indian friend over the telephone how they managed to kill their Prime Minister."

"And so?" the judge asked.

"And so we think he is planning some evil against the Prime Minister."

18)

The woman had taken the Fulani man to court for spying on her as she was bathing naked behind her house.

"Why did you do that?" the judge asked.

"Eye no get boundary, sa," the man replied.

19)

"Why did you break the chair on your husband's head?" the judge asked the woman who had been brought before him for wounding her husband during a domestic scuffle.

"Sorry, your worship. I did not mean to break the chair. It was the idiot's head that I really wanted to scatter."

20)

The officer was definitely very excited with his achievement which made him an instant celebrity. He had single-handedly caught six armed robbers sharing their loot.

"And how did you manage to catch all of them?" a colleague of his asked.

"I surrounded them at once with my gun," he said. Actually he meant surrendered.

21)

The day was the eve of the Students' Union Elections, and Joshua an immensely popular students was hoping to become the Social Welfare Officer (S.W.O.). After a rousing fifty-minute speech he was carried shoulder high by his mates, marched the distance of three kilometres round the college campus, and then taken to his bed. He was then fanned until he fell asleep.

The following day, when the votes were counted, Joshua had only one vote. That means even those who carried him round the campus did not votes. Each person thought the other would vote for him. Politics is dirty, at any level.

22)

The reputation of the government and its Ministers was extremely low, and with good reason. To respond to a public interview, the questions needed to be given to them a week in advance so that they prepare and rehearse the answers before appearing on TV. All this was supposed to be a secret.

But on one occasion a Minister gave the secret away when he started answering a question before it was asked. Then he tried to correct himself:

"Sorry, that is the answer to question four.

Can you repeat the question please?"

23)

Another Minister completely confused the order of the answers, giving the answer to the question on constitutional reforms to that on possible methods to be adopted for land reclamation and avoiding brain-drain.

24)

A Minister of Transport came to inaugurate a new bridge. After reading only three pages of a twelve-page speech, as he shuffled the third sheet under the pile to turn to the fourth sheet, the poorly stapled sheets fell out of his hands into the river. The speech had been written by somebody else. Needless to say the ceremony ended prematurely as he stammered to say:

"We are all happy that before the forces of nature intervened, with this ceremony, the bridge had long been complete."

The crowd cheered as he cut the tape.

25)

"You must seize all the copies of the newspaper from every student," the Chief of Public Security told the Head of the University.

Campus Security concerning a certain viciously frank opposition newspaper that had been published in the university.

"What's the point seizing the papers, sir?" the man asked.

"The students have all read the paper. The information is all in their heads now."

"And what's wrong with cutting off the heads of those who have it?' the man enquired modestly.

26)

The part in power had fallen into disrepute, such that nobody was anxious to march in the uniforms of the party on the National Day. To give the impression of continuous popularity, the party organisers distributed party uniforms to prisoners whom they compelled to march, singing party songs. But as soon as the prisoners reached the end of the march they escaped to freedom, uniforms and all.

27)

The Mayor came personally to ask the police to release his delinquent son.

"This boy is not as bad as you think," he said as he signed the papers for the boy's release "people just continue to tell bad stories against him to soil my reputation," he went on.

The policeman opened the door, the boy came out, dressed and was just about to enter his father's car and be driven away when one of the inmates shouted:

"Please check Joe's things properly. The shirt his is wearing is mine."

They called him back and started questioning him. None of the items he had just put on belonged to him.

28)

Corporal Abam had been served with a retirement notice; one morning Sergeant Kombo of the Equipment Division showed up at Corporal Abam's door to collect his kit.

"Corporal no. 880," the sergeant said.

"Yes sep."

"Your kit."

After running round the house for ten minutes he began handing over the things as they were being spelled out; But two items were missing: a black pair of trousers and a singlet.

"Those do not exist," the man said. "I have looked all over the house." Just then the Sergeant's orderly went up to the corporal and whispered something in his ears.

The corporal looked at his singlet and trousers. They were the very ones that were being demanded.

"I will die with this one," corporal Abam said.

"I give this and I remain naked."

29)

A man had come from the village to have the Police Commissioner's signature on his documents. He arrived the police station who the detainees had been taken out to bask in to noonday sun. He did not know who they were and did not ask any questions; Soon afterwards the officer on duty shouted to the detainees:

"All man go insite!"

The man followed the detainees inside and it was only when the door was locked behind him that he noticed that he had been mistaken for a detainee.

30)

"You see, sir," the detainee was telling the officer how he came to be arrested. "The man from whom I wanted to borrow the money was sleeping. But he woke up before I could remove my hand from his pocket. So people began to say I am a thief, that I am a thief.

Just see that kind of thing!"

31)

The lady of the house had gone to the village and stayed there for one week. She was questioning her young son about things that happened in her absence.

"One night we had a terrible thunderstorm, I was so afraid that I ran and met daddy and we slept together."

"Yes," the house girl supported. "That was on Monday."

"Lies," the little boy shouted. "It was on Sunday. On Monday night was it not you and daddy who slept?"

32)

"This party is not for Intellectuals as people have claimed," the man was trying to defend his party platform. "It is for the masses;"

"Okay," somebody said. "Show one mass amongst us here who is your supporter."

33)

An Englishman who was led to the archives of the Ministry of Finance was amazed by the jumbled nature of the files.

"why don't you try to put some order in the arrangement of these files? It must take you a lifetime to trace a document if you needed to," the man said.

"That is true, sir," said the keeper of the archives. "But these is a reason why we mix things up like this. We Africans are very wicked people. When the things are mixed up like this and somebody is looking for your document to destroy it and make you suffer, he will not see it in time."

34)

The man was accused of leaking the party secrets to opponents. He did not deny the accusation.

"You don't make me look like I have done the worst thing in this world," he said. "Look at Christ. He had only twelve disciples, and one of them was a traitor. I am only one out of one million members of this party, and you want to kill me!"

35)

The people remember the incident as the most wicked act to be conceived by a gendarme. A vehicle knocked down a child. As a passing taximan stopped to help the child to the hospital the Gendarme ordered the taximan not to touch the bleeding child until the police had written their on-the-spot report.

36)

"The object of this treaty," said the Canadian Ambassador, "is to build a bridge between Yaounde and Ottawa;"

he was of course speaking metaphorically, but the Mayor took it literally.

"Instead of spending money on such an expensive venture," the Mayor said, when it came to his turn, 'the Canadian Government should just help us to tar the roads in our capital city here."

37)

A thief once broke into the hospital safe and stole money and very valuable documents.

"There is an instant reward of 500,000 francs for anybody who gives information leading to the capture of the thief," radio announcement said.

Two days later the thief went up to the radio to claim the reward.

38)

During the early days of Idi Amin's reign in Uganda, soldiers were asked to search the homes of suspected Obote supporters. They entered the study of a university lecturer and pointing to his library of some 2000 books asked.

"What do you have in those books?"

The man was, accordingly, arrested for concealing information about his books.

39)

The soldiers had taken the law into their hands and had begun looting and seizing the property of civilians. On one pretext or another they would confiscate property. The pet question was the demand for the receipts of property. The civilians therefore did everything to hide their belongings at their approach. One night, returning home late, after all the stations had closed a man was told that soldiers might be raiding his area that night. He immediately carried his large radio outside and hid it in garbage under a plantain stem. The soldiers made their usual rounds, found nothing of value to carry away. At about five o'clock in the morning they began making their way back to the barracks. Suddenly, from under the garbage the national anthem was being played. The national station was about to resume broadcast.

40)

The soldiers were even said to have taken away a man's beautiful wife on the grounds that he could not produce the receipt for owning the woman.

41)

All the Parliamentarians from the Northern Province had been told to remain solidly behind their son, the Prime Minister. If he clapped they were also to clap without seeking to understand why.

At the Parliamentary session it worked twice. But the third time, as he tried to kill a fly that was disturbing him, the observant Parliamentarians clapped for give minutes, to the utter embarrassment of everybody else.

42)

The learned Professor entered the Police Station fuming to report that his car had been stolen. The Officer on duty asked him to write down the complaint.

He carefully wrote down exactly what had happened to the police. The car had suddenly stalled, a passer-by had offered to help: he had examined the car and had entered in and asked the Professor to give it a push. As soon as the car had started the passer-by had driven the car away.

"Did you look at his identity card to know his name, tribe, and so on?"

"When you are in trouble and somebody comes to help, do you ask for his identification papers?"

"Then, perhaps the Professor thinks we of the police force are magicians. You give your car keys to an unknown passer-by, you open the door for him to go in, you help him push the car, and when he goes away you come to the police to go and catch him."

43)

"What do you say about this student unrest?" the journalist asked the illiterate Minister of Education.

"How can they rest?" he asked. "Library back to dormitory, to class, and so on. They cannot rest."

44)

In the wake multipartism in Cameroon, a journalist asked one of the mushroom party leaders:

"Mr. Chairman, what are your impressions about this burning issue of Federation of the two states of this country?"

"I be never support**Federal no one day. That thing de spoil carburettor over. It has spoiled me three Land-rovers."

45)

A magistrate travelling from Nkongsamba to Bamenda stopped at Nkombu to buy meat when he overheard a conversation between two thieves who were leading a gang. He rode ahead of the gang and at the Santa police check-point he called the head of the officers on duty.

"There is a gang of armed robbers coming this way. They should be here within the next hour. Do everything to arrest them. I am going ahead to ask for reinforcement." Accordingly the Magistrate proceeded to the Commissioner for Pubic Security to whom he told the story. The Commissioner immediately mobilised 15 strong men and headed for the Santa check-point. But when they got there they found that the policemen on duty had not

(Federal in Cameroon is the name given to illegally imported petrol from neighbouring Nigeria) only deserted their post but had pulled down the flimsy road-blocks mounted to check taximen and tax defaulters.

46)

A contingent of Gendarmes was sent to quell a village rebellion. The following Sunday one of them, a God-fearing gentlemen went to Church. During communion he rose and went to the altar. On his return he noticed from the distance that his cap which he left on his eat had been taken away.

"Let the man who has taken my cap put it right back!" he shouted.

"Sssssssshhhhh!" the catchiest said, putting his fore-finger to his lips.

"Won't you even finish the communion in your mouth?"

"Ssssssshhhh for what?" the Gendarme asked. "If they do not produce the cap nobody is leaving this bar!"

47)

A notorious goat thief once took a cord and wrapped round his neck and then ran from once end of the village to the other shouting:

"Today will be the last day you see me; I am going to kill myself." People who heard and saw him remained silent, some even rejoiced. A few minutes later the man came running back towards the other end of the village shouting:

"Those of you who hate me will see. When you did not stop me, you thought I was going to die. God has refused. I see what you will do to me. Wicked people like you."

7

MAN DIE NA DIE

1)

The man, originally from Bafia, was travelling from Douala to Yaounde on a business tour when he was robbed of his brief case as he struggle to enter the train. The thief jumped from the speedy train. But nobody in the train noticed that he had not been all that lucky, for when he fell he rolled back on to the rails and was instantly crushed.

All that the railway workers later found was a partially destroyed brief case lying by the shattered limbs and mangled body. When they opened the brief case and found the passport of the deceased, a radio announcement was immediately made inviting friends and relatives to report to the hospital for the remains of Mr. Evon Martin which had been preserved in the fridge in the Douala mortuary.

The "bundle' was eventually collected and taken to his home town for burial. The business man had to cut short his visit to Yaounde because he had lost the bag containing all his documents for the trip. Back in Douala he learned what people thought had happened to him. After telling them what had actually happened he rushed to his village to tell the people the truth. Very much alive, he arrived Bafia at the tail end of the funeral rites. Friends and relatives and other sympathisers fled into the bush as soon as they saw him. And why not? Who would confront a ghost?

2)

A severed head lying in the gutter immediately after a road accident exclaimed;"

"Massa, if not he help of God I would have died."

3)

"How are things?" a neighbour asked the undertaker.

"Not moving at all. Not moving?"

"why, you are sick,"

"No. For two months now, nobody has died in this quarter."

4)

"Is there anything you would like to say before they finish you?" the hangman asked the notorious armed robber.

"Yes," the man said.

"What?"

"A fire extinguisher," he said. Then he murmured to himself; " I will see how that your hell that everybody is talking about will touch me."

5)

On some other occasion the hangman asked another victim if he had anything to say before they killed him.

"Yes," the man said. "I want to say that my enemies should live long to see what I will become."

6)

Still with the hangman, a certain Akpan had been sentenced to death for murdering his half-brother, Edet, whom he had allegedly caught making love to his wife **on his own bed**.

"Dou you have anything to say before they kill yu?" the hang man asked in the customary fashion.

"I get only let Edt know that the thing he do me so bad that even after this, to say I meet him again, whether in heaven or in hell, I go still kill him very many times."

7)

Pa Wandak came home to hear that a notorious school teacher had slipped into his house with his very young wife. When he pushed the door it was locked.

"Emilia, Emilia," he called.

No answer. That confirmed the suspicious.

"I will give you people bad luck for shaming me," he said.

His house was situated on the edge of a ravine. He took a rope and went behind the house and attached to a timber that overlooked the ravine. He made a loop and put over his head and swung from over the edge to die as a sign of protest against his wife's misconduct; The roof followed him into the ravine. And by the time rescuers go him out of the danger, it was difficult to convince them about why he had tried to do that because the young teacher had fled.

8)

The following telegram was received in the London hospital where a man who was finally buried in Cameroon had died.

"Le cadavre est arrivé en bon santé." Meaning literally that the corpse arrived in good health.

9)

An octogenarian called for his son and asked him to throw away a blanket he had used for some twenty years. He had just bought a new one.

The blanket on hearing this said:

"No way. I have helped you for twenty years, if you want to throw me away, know that I will go with you."

That night, the old man died, and true to the blanket's prediction, he was wrapped and buried in the old blanket.

10)

At a funeral in Ngomo, an elderly neighbour thought he had been treated with disrespect. The neighbours, knowing him to be very weak at alcohol were not anxious to ruin the ceremony by giving him too much to drink.

"What does this mean?" the man asked. "Am I the one who said Sam should die? I sit here for one hour, no beer, you only select the people to whom to give drinks. Let another death occur in this house and you see if I will put my foot here."

The host answered him:

"So you think death will be coming only to this house, not so? It will not come to your house because you think we work in a mortuary here? When you yourself die we shall see who will be there."

11)

A God-fearing Bamileke man invited his three sons to his bedside as he lay dying.

"I leave all the business here in your hands," he said, "to go ahead to prepare the way for you people. But I ask for something. There is life after death as the church says. It will therefore be a good thing for me to start business again there while waiting for you. When I die, I want each of you to put one million francs in each pocket of my coat before you seal the coffin."

When he died the first two brothers did exactly as their father had requested. The third hesitated when he went in to pay his last respects to his father.

"If it is true that there is business over there," he reflected, " then their banking system must be excellent."

He pulled out the two million francs which his brothers had put in their father's pockets and wrote out a check for three million francs which he put in there and walked out.

12)

"I hate to die this kind of death," a man said, referring to a ghastly accident in which the victim was shattered beyond recognition.

13)

Frustrated in business a man took a rope to hang himself. But as he climbed a tree he saw a snake. Abandoning the rope he jumped down and fled back home.

14)

Another man who had climbed up a tree in the night to hang himself noticed a hunter pointing a gun in his direction:
"Don't do like that and shoot me-eh!" he shouted.

15)

A very prominent business man had just died, and it was rumoured that he had left instructions in his will that there would be a crate of beer for each mourner or sympathiser at the funeral. A neighbour was just cleaning his drinking cup to go and mourn for the great man when news came to him that his own sister had died.

"Make them put the die body for fridge for mortuary," the man said. "I want to attend a correct die first; Die no de pass some?"

16)

A woman whose husband lay sick of cancer once ordered a very expensive and eye-catching mourning garment. But for two years she could not wear it because nobody died whom she knew.

Finally the man was declared healed. Still bent on wearing the garment, she went to the hospital and asked the man on duty:

"Has anybody died today?"

"Are you controlling deaths?" an insolent nurse asked.

"No, I just wanted to know," she said.

"Go to the mortuary and find out," the nurse told her.

To the mortuary she went. There were ten corpses inside.

"Do you know their addresses?" she asked the keeper of the mortuary.

"Just send the letter to hell, they will get it," the man said. "They are three policemen and a Gendarmerie."

17)

A corpse was being transported from the hospital to a waiting vehicle on a stretcher, when one of the men bearing the stretcher hit his foot against a stone and fell. As he dragged down the stretcher the corpse rolled over and fell off.

"Terrible thing," one of the relatives of the deceased cried. "They will just kill me this my brother completely."

18)

A plantation worker who loved his drink actually died from excess alcohol. Because the Corporation stored ready-made coffins, the relatives went for one. But as they lowered the corpse into it they discovered that the coffin was too long, and that there was much space left to the upper end.

"We need to put something in there t keep the body inside from rolling up and down," one of the relatives pointed out. Somebody measured the space left and nodded.

"If Joe will like to get up down there and see anything, it should be beer," he said. "That space is good enough to take a crate of 33 Export bee."

19)

An old man married to two very young wives lay dying when he was visited by the father of the younger wife.

"My brother," the visitor began, "how can you do this to us? You want to go now and leave my daughter in whose hands?"

"Don't worry," the dying man said. " I am not leaving any of them behind. I am going with everybody."

20)
"DEAD BUT NOT FORGIVEN", was the caption on the board that the family had ordered to be put over the grave of their beloved father.

It was an error in translation because the man who gave the artist the message had said FORGIVEN, which meant the same as FORGOTTEN, in the dialect.

21)
Our colleague had lost his sister-in-law, and since he was such a good friend of ours, we had decided to show him how much we cared about him. We each brought a crate of Becks beer, four crates altogether, and our wives brought two large flasks of food.

We delivered the items and sat back sharing in the loss. The carefully washed flasks were just being returned when our friend, looking at the pictures on the walls called one of the people and asked:

"Who died here? Was it not mama Angelina?"

"No sa," the woman said. "Mama Angelina's death is in the next compound. But we also have our own here. Where are here for sister Sophie's death."

"What is happening?" I asked.

"We have missed the compound," he said with self-bitterness.

There was no way of retrieving anything we had brought because the choir, each member with a bottle of Becks beer in hand, had begun signing songs in priase of our generosity.

22)
The entire Primary School had turned up to condole with the Headmaster who had just lost his only son, a pupil of that institution.

"Look at how man children there are in this school," the man cried, unable to contain his emotion. "And death chooses only my own child…"

"You wanted it to take whose child?" an angry parent asked.

23)

The polygamist with four wives had just received news that his favourite wife had died in an accident.

"Papa God," he cried, forgetting for awhile those standing by him. "why did you not ask me which woman to give you?"" he asked;

"You would have given who?" the others asked all at the same time.

24)

Another polygamist addressed God on the loss of his beautiful wife:

"Papa God, you leave all these dirty rags in the house and choose only my golden egg?

Why?"

It was no surprise that all the others packed out of his house leaving him alone to mourn for his golden egg.

25)

"Oh lala!" the man shouted in the bar.

"All those who have died must be regretting now. See how cheap the price of alcohol has become."

26)

A man had just died and the next-of-kin was taking stock of the deceased's debts when the leader of the dead man's orchestra said:

"He was owing us three months pay.

"Where is the receipt?" the stock-taker enquired.

27)

"Why have only one piece of meat in his soup, while the other people have two each?"

a customer asked the servant in a local restaurant.

"Sorry, na mistake sa," the man customer and cut the piece of meat into two pieces.

28)

A man once met his father-in-law in the bar to whom he offered a bottle of beer. He himself asked for a piece of chicken. The father-in-law took two sips and then asked the man:

"You give me beer and you yourself you take beef, so if the beer tight for my throat I will use what to swallow it down?"

29)

"At last they are together," a neighbour said outside the compound in which a popular girl had died.

"Did she die because some relative or husband died before?" a sympathizer enquired.

"Or you mean they who?"

"Her legs," the neighbour added. "When this girl was alive I never knew that her legs will ever close. She opened them everywhere she went."

8

MARRETTE: FOR BUTTER OR FOR WAX

"What God has put together let no man push pass Under."

1)

A man who had beaten his wife and asked her to leave his house was surprised to see her taking their little 5-year old boy. "Where are you going with my child?" he shouted.

"It's not your child," she said. "This is the son of Lucas."

"Which Lucas? The houseboy I sent away?"

"Yes" she admitted boldly

2)

The wedding went exactly as planned, very successfully. Friends and relatives gathered from both sides were in attendance. First the best friend of the groom spoke, reviewing his past in glowing terms, saying how lucky Elsie must be to be married to such a boy.

Then came the turn of the best friend of the bride.

"We always wondered," she began, "whether this girl would ever get married. She never spoke to a boy, never went out of their house as soon as she returned from school; never attended parties like the rest of us. I want to tell Phyl that he is lucky to be married to this virgin."

But it would appear the mother of Elsie was too busy preparing her speech to listen to what her daughter's friend was saying.

'The most important thing in marriage," she began when it came to her turn, "is having children. If a woman is as good as what, if she is married and does not have any children; she is useless; and the marriage will not work.

I want to tell Philip that if they get into this marriage and they do not have any children, then it is his fault because my daughter is from family that delivers. Before Elsie was 15 years old, she already had a child. If you look at the girl, you will even think that she is only her sister."

3)

A man walked into the American Life Insurance Company in Bamenda and asked:

"Do you ensure marriages?"

"You mean insure marriages how?" the agent asked.

"That is, if my wife leaves my house, I can come and claim some money."

"We shall try to include that in our programme," the agent said.

"If only that will not give you the licence to beat your wife away in order to claim your insurance."

4)

"The man I will marry has got to be versatile," the university graduate was telling her friends. "He must be able to sing, to dance, to tell stories, to play football, to cheer me up when I am sad, to do anything I enjoy seeing…"

"Then you want to marry a television set," a listener told her.

5)

"It is all worked out," the retired ambassador was telling the young man about the marriage arrangements of his daughters.

"Anna is 19," he went on. "She is my angel.

We think that 300,000francs will not be asking for too much from anybody like you."

The young man nodded.

"Josephine is twenty-five," the old man went on. "Any suitor should be ready to give us at least 200,000francs."

The man nodded.

"Patricia is already catching up with us. She is 35, but she is a wonderful creature. Very serviceable. For 100,000francs we would readily part with her."

The young man nodded, reflected for a whole minute and then asked:

"Pa, do you have anyone who is about forty or forty-five?"

6)

To hurt his stubborn wife a man bought a poppy and called it Patience, his wife's name.

She retorted by buying a pig and calling it Stephen.

"Have you ever seen a pig with such a long name?" he asked.

"Then where did you get that one from?" she asked.

7)

Any connection?" the Pastor asked, as a matter of formality. The young man zho had come to register his marriage had just given his names as Alum Martinus,a and the girl had given hers as Martinus Feh.

There was a minute of silence, during which the prospective couple exchanged glances.

Then the girl whispered to the boy:

"Tell him, after all are we not going to get married?"

"Yes, Pastor," the boy said hesitatingly.

"Twice only," he said. "We have had two connections, but that was only because we knew we were going to get married."

8)

This reminds us of the girl in Chinua Achebe's novel who was given a form to fill out at an interview. When she came to the column:

SEX, she wrote "twice a week."

On another occasion a boy wrote "six inches."

9)

The people were discussing the advantages of marrying in church.

"I married in court," one said.

"It means you missed the only opportunity for your wife to put food in your mouth with her own hand," the other said.

10)

"At an occasion like this one," the eloquent M.C of the wedding began, "there's got to be sacrifice, cash as well as kind." He turned on the video and continued; pointing to the screen:

"See what common animals have done to make this occasion successful. See how many animals have been willing to lose their lives, just so that we can have a good marriage..."

11)

A man who introduced a girl to his friend as his future wife was shocked the following week to find the two in a very compromising situation.

"Don't tell me you are doing that to my future wife," he shouted.

"You said your future wife," the man said.

"You needed her for the future but I needed her for now."

12)

A young man took his girl friend to an erotic film in order to excite her sexually. When they were leaving the hall, the girl said:

"You see how white men sleep and make with their women? If it were you you would be snoring like a pig."

"You can say so," the boy responded, "because you don't know that those people are paid to be doing all that. Pay me the amount of money they pay them, and I shall see whether I will not break your waist house."

13)

The M.C. was thanking all those who had contributed in one way or the other to make the event so successful. He went through a long list and finally said:

"I cannot end without thanking myself for lending Mike the suit and the shoes which he is wearing."

14)

"I'll give you a ring," the young man just coming from London told the girl at the party, implying that he would call her on the phone the next day.

"That your brother is terrible," the girl went and said to the been-to's sister early the very next morning.

"Why?"

"He just sees me today and plans to marry me tomorrow!"

15)

"What would happen if your husband came in and met us doing this?" the adulterer asked.

"The fool, what will he do?" the unfaithful wife asked. Just then the husband who was supposed to have travelled pushed the door, came in and saw a man on his wife.

"What are you people doing like that?" the husband shouted.

"I told you," the woman said." He does not even know what we are doping."

16)

The couple had agreed that they would make love only on those days of the week in which there was an R in the spelling: that is to say, Saturday, Thursday, Friday. The man on journey and returned two weeks afterwards on Sunday night. They had a restless night. O Monday night, when the man asked the woman what day of the week it was, she told him:

"MonRay."

17)

"Something terrible is going on in that Christian Women's Fellowship," the man said to his friend over the phone.

"What has happened?"

"My wife has just returned with a packet of ten condoms. If that is what they go to learn in that place, I will never allow her to go there again. Did your wife not go there?"

"She went," the man replied. "Let me ask her."

After five minutes he returned to tell his friend:

"My wife says they were actually given fourteen condoms each."

The receiver fell from the man's hands.

18)

The disloyal husband's marriage was threatened. He had returned late, wearing his shirt inside out, and the wife swore she would take it no more. The ingenious man rang up his friend and explained the situation to him.

The man to whom the matter had been reported drove over to the friend's house and knocked at the door

"Is he in?"The man asked.

"Who?" the woman asked

"My friend."

"The cow is sleeping in bed."

"Was he able to get his shirt?"

"From where?"

"Thieves attacked him and were dragging him all over the place," the man tried to defend his friend.

"And when they left him," the woman began, "they tied a woman's underpants to his waist?"

The problem was more serious than the man thought before he feigned sleep.

19)

Did you hear of the man who hired a photographer for their wedding celebration and they returned after 36 poses only to find that the man had forgotten the films at home?

They had been posing to an empty camera?

20)

The man had received the news of the wife's death with very great relief because he had suffered too much in her hands. But just two days afterwards, as he entered his room, her late wife's handbag which had been precariously placed on the edge of a shelf fell and wounded his forehead;

"I knew that whether in heaven or in hell this woman will never let me sleep quiet in his house," he said.

21)

A carpenter who specialised in the making of huge cupboards married a very unfaithful wife. Each time he went out the woman would bring her lover into their home.

He return home very unexpectedly with a man who had ordered a cupboard to be made for him. When he entered his bedroom he suspected something. He had the feeling that his wife had just been in there with a man, that the man had not left the room, and that he was most likely in the cupboard.

He immediately locked the cupboard and put the keys in his pocket, and for the church.

During the offertory he donated the keys.

After service the pastor enquired:

"Who gave these keys?"

"I did," the man said.

"What are they for?"

"They are the keys of a cupboard in my house. I want to give it to God."

Four strong men were selected to go for the cupboard which the man described as very heavy. The cupboard was dragged to the church and as it was opened for the admiration of the congregation, a naked pastor emerged from inside.

22)

A young man working in a city wrote back to the village asking his parents to look for and send him a young girl, a virgin, for marriage.

His request was granted. But just after one night with her he discovered that she was no stranger to men. He parcelled her back to his parents with the note:

"Good damaged before delivery, return bride price."

23)

"How many wives have you?" the master asked his night watch.

"Two sa," the man replied, and then as he saw his master wondering he asked:

"Why is patron wondering? Is this not a bilingual country?"

114

9

OVASABY – SENSE – PASS – KING

1)

"What is your name? Where do you come from?" the old man shouted at the boy he had just caught harvesting and destroying his unripe mangoes.

"Don't tell him your name, Francis, he will go and report us to papa," said the boy's little brother.

2)

"I will not split wood in this rain," said the man who had just been employed to work in the compound.

"Why?" the lady of the house asked. "The rain is not even serious.

"When the rain is falling I cannot spit in my palm and hold the axe," the man said.

3)

A notorious criminal took a rope and ran from one end of the village to the other, shouting:

"I de go hand, I de go die'ooh! Wona hold me'ooh!"

but nobody interrupted him. When he had reached the end of the village he began walking back defying the entire community:

"Na so wona hate me. Man say I de go die man no hol'am. I go hard wona. I no go die, no one day."

115

4)

In a folktale a fox, pretending it was dead, and hoping to have a hare for its meal, lay near the entrance into the cave where a hare lived.

The hare came out, took one look at the fox and nodded. He knew it was a trap.

"My husband is dead," the fox's wife sobbed.

"I don't think so," said the hare.

"Why don't you think so?" asked Mrs. Fox.

"When a fox dies," the hare went on, "its hands are placed on its chest."

On hearing this, and to emphasize the fact that it was very dead, the fox placed its hands on its chest.

"Yes," said the hare. "You will die again."

5)

There is also the story of Mr. Tiger who fell into a pit and would have died had a monkey not come by and lowered its tail, by the help of which the tiger got out.

"You know that for all these days that I was in this pit I have had nothing to eat?" the tiger asked the monkey the monkey soon after it had saved his life.

"So what should I do?" the monkey asked.

"Should I go and look for food for you?"

"Go and look for food? I cannot wait that long," the tiger said. "I want to eat you."

The monkey was still pleading when a tortoise came by. After the monkey had examined what had happened the tortoise said:

"I don't believe a word of what you are saying. That a small monkey like you can lift a tiger from the pit just by lowering your tail."

When the monkey insisted that the tiger was correct, the tortoise said:

"O.K, do it again. If you really succeed, I shall agree with the tiger that you be eaten."

The tiger jumped back into the hole and asked the monkey to lower the tail again.

"Don't do it," the tortoise said. "When somebody helps you, you must thank him, not eat him."

"But I had thanked him already," said the tiger. "Ask him."

6)

A man who felt that he had begun to lose his potency went to a medicine man and complained. The man took 25,000 francs from his customer and then gave him the thing that would do the trick: a bundle of jigija, a cord of multi-coloured beads to tie round his waist every time he wanted to make love to his wife.

"Then how do explain the presence of such things round my waist?" the embarrassed man asked.

"You want your thing to stand or to know what people would ask?"

7)

It is like the story of a boy who went to another medicine man.

"I want something to charm women with," he said. "Do you have it?"

Of course, the man had whatever it is he wanted. The fee, which he promptly paid, was 1,000 francs. But it was how to administer it that created a problem.

"Just rob'am for the woman I forehead," the medicine man said. "Any place you go, I go follow you."

"What will it look like, seeing me walk up to a woman and rob her face?"

8)

Multipartism did not come easily to Cameroon. The government did everything in its power to frustrate aspiring political leaders. There is a case, for example, of a man who submitted the name of his party too the Minister of Territorial Administration for endorsement. The Minister refused to sign. His reasons:

"You must submit along with your application to form a party the list of the members of your party."

A prospective opposition leader went away and the following week he held a rally. He was arrested for causing disorder.

"Did I not tell you not to organised any political rally until you had produced the names of your party members?" the Minister asked.

"You did," the man replied.

"And have you produced the list?"

"When a doctor wants to open a clinic do you ask him to first produce the names of all the patients he would admit in his unopened clinic," the man enquired. "Or if a man who has applied to open a bar do you first ask him to produce a list of those who will be drinking in it."

9)

"Let's leave the stupid fool alone," the man leading the fruitless and exhausting pursuit of a pickpocket said when the thief disappeared into a nearby bush and hid himself.

"Who are you calling a stupid fool?" the thief shouted from the bush.

10)

"I protect my property too well," a man said in the bar. "No thief can get into my house."

Some thieves had overheard him boasting and late the following night, they visited him.

When he heard people moving things in his parlour the opened a big box and hid inside.

Having found nothing of value in the parlour to take away the thieves entered the room and decided to carry away the box. As they dragged the box the man cried and threw it open.

"What are you doing in the box?" one of the thieves asked.

"I was ashamed because there was nothing in my house for you to take away, that is why I hid myself inside," said the man.

11)

It is like the thief who broke into a student's bedroom and began searching for valuables.

He managed to drag a huge box from under the bed and open it without making any noise. There was nothing inside, except books. He succeeded in destroying the key to the boy's cupboard and when he opened it, he found only books. Frustrated he shook the boy out of sleep and asked:

"When you hide only books everywhere like this, what do you expect us the poor people to eat?"

The boy had not replied when he gave him a slap in the face and then walked out and away.

12)

A hungry and thirsty school-boy came across a sugar-cane farm, but he could not touch anything there because there was medicine hanging all over the place. Determined to harvest some the boy untied a goat that was grazing in the nearby farm and then tied it to one of the sugar-canes. He then whipped the goat and followed it until he sugar-cane fell out of the rope. The medicine could not affect him.

13)

A man was returning from a stream with basket full of tadpoles he had caught to make supper for his family when he found two hares sleeping side-by-side in the banks of a river. He immediately dropped the tadpoles in the river and then ran home.

"Wash the biggest pot in this house," he told his wife. "I am going to bring real meat."

By the time he returned to the scene the animals had long gone.

14)

Another version of the story has it that a man was passing through the forest when he saw an antelope that had been caught in a trap. He cut down leaves which he spread on the ground, sat down and worked out how he was going to cut up the animal and noted down the names of those who would receive particular parts. When that was done he walked up to the antelope and as soon as he lifted the cutlass the animal jumped from where it was lying and he struck and cut the wire that held the animal. It fled.

15)

To cope with the mounting economic crises, the government sought strange ways of raising revenue. One such way was to impose a licence on windscreens. Every vehicle owner was to pay for it and obtain a sticker. The police stopped a certain man and asked for the windscreen licence.

"I don't even have a windscreen," the man said, having deliberately taken it off to avoid the tax: the windscreen cost 15,000francs.

"You pay so that when you buy a windscreen you put this sticker on it," said the police.

16)

It is like the story of the man who showed up in the office with only one hand. The previous week a priceless item had been stolen from the safe in the office and it was said the day from London to check out the workers. He wanted to get even with the expert." I will see how they will take my fingerprint," the man thought.

17)

My first novel sold for 2,000francs immediately after publication. The publishers decided to lower the price, clear the stock and print a second edition. The book then was sold for 1,000francs. When a customer heard of the reduction in price he said:

"Since the price falls every six months, I shall buy the book after three years so that I pay only 200 francs."

18)

The college driver wrote to the principal threatening him with resignation in two weeks, unless he received a pay raise.

The principal hired a new driver rather than increase the pay. When the driver heard of the Principal's decision he returned.

"I was just joking, Father," he said. "I beg you to take me back."

"There was no way of telling that it was a joke," the principal said. "If you want to work here again, then I will pay you what I would have paid the new man."

The new man was to receive 5,000francs less than what the driver received originally.

"O.K., father," he accepted!

19)

The boy had been told to pretend he was deaf and dumb and he would not be harassed for travelling without a valid passport. His friend was to be with him everywhere they went, to announce his infirmity to the policeman. At the Cameroon-Nigeria border, as he sat unmoved an impatient policeman slapped him. "You slap who like that?" he shouted at the policeman.

20)

Another version of the story says that the policeman told his colleague.

"That boy sitting there looks like the boy who robbed that woman here last week!"

"It cannot be me," the supposedly deaf and dumb shouted. "This is my first time of passing through here."

21)

In a similar case, a diminutive man carried two cards with him to explain his problem. The blue card read:

OKAFOR WAS BORN DEAF AND DUMB. ANYTHING YOU GIVE WILL HELP HIM.

There was also the white card bearing the same information, but translated into French. He strolled into a music shop one day and looked at the people who were conversing and sorted the cards. He then gave the blue card to those who were speaking in English and then the white to those who spoke French. One of the people examined the card for a long time and then asked:

"Who has put these cards here?"

Okarfor walked up to him, showed the man the board and twenty big cities in the world.

"That is the only place I have not gone to," the man told him.

23)

Vehicles and the train used the same bridge.

The railway tracks ran through the middle of the road while traffic passed on either side. It was rush time and cars were moving bumper to bumper when a taxi man decided to get out of the queue. The gap he left closed behind him at once. He had hardly driven 20 yards when he sighted the train coming qt breakneck speed. He could not rejoin the line, so he abandoned his car in the train's track and escaped.

24)

"I came here to take care of the problems my brother has left behind," the man said to the widow of his brother.

"Go ahead," she said.

"I want to see his bank book," the man said.

"I don't know here he kept it," she said.

"But I know the account number."

The man asked for it and the next minute he was talking to the bank manager.

"I came here as the next of kin to take care of my brother's problems. I want to start with his money," he said.

"Fine," the manager said , and gave him a form to fill, which he did. They then took his identification papers and went in to consult their records. After ten minutes the manager called for the man and told him:

"People like you are very rare.

"Why rare? The man asked. "How much money did he leave behind?"

"Nothing. In fact we are glad you came because he was owing the bank 500,000francs, and we were just wondering how we were going to recover such money."

"I came because he was owing," the man said.

25)

"This is all rubbish," the old French professor cursed, tearing apart his copy of the Divine Comedy. "How could Dante be so stupid, so ignorant as not say anything about Moliere or Voltaire?"

Of course we all know that the French writers he was referring to were born some 500 years after Dante!

26)

"Did you shout for help?" a man asked his wife who had just told him that her meat-seller had raped her.

"I didn't," she replied.

"Why?" he asked.

"Because he promised me another kilogramme of meat."

27)

A woman walked up to a blind man and, opening her purse pulled out a 1,000francs note and handed over to him. As she walked away a pickpocket approached her from behind and put his hand into her handbag.

"Heh!" the blind man shouted. "Why do you want to steal that woman's money?

"Did you not say you were blind?" the thief asked him.

"Who well?" the blind-man asked.

28)

Upon hearing that the world was going to end the following day, a man went to the bank, withdrew all his money and entered a shop.

"I want to buy everything in here," he said.

"Why? Do you need all that?" the shop-keeper asked.

"I don't really need it. Just that I want to spend all my money. "They say the world ends tomorrow."

"Then you take me for a fool?" the shopkeeper asked. "The world is coming to an end, and you want to take my goods in exchange for your papers? Take them away."

29)

A man caught stealing a goat pretended to be dumb. He was, however, taken to court. He brought along his own witnesses.

"Are you sure this man is really dumb?" the judge asked.

"I swear it," one of the thief's witnesses said.

"All that you are saying enters one ear and passes through the other."

"Let him be wasting his time asking me the same question," the thief said to his friend, thus betraying himself.

The town decided to put a fence round their cemetery. One man would not. Dragged to the District Officer for refusal to do community work the man defended himself:

"I don't see why we should build the fence."
The people in the graves can't come out.
Those of us outside here can't go in."

30)

"Why do you serve me such shall food? Look at how much you have given the man at the door, and he has paid the same price," the man complained, who had just chanced on a restaurant.

"We served him like that to attract customers," the steward said.

31)

"The job is only for people with a bachelor's degree," the personnel manager shouted at the applicant. "It is not for bachelors!"

32)

during the Second World War, the British tried to appeal to Africans to join the allied forces against Hitler. Said one British Officer to an African Chieftain during the extensive propaganda campaign against the Naw's:

"Away with Hitler! Down with him!"

"What has he done?" asked the African chieftain.

"He wants to rule the whole world," the officer said.

"What's wrong with that?"

"He is a German," the Officer said; trying to appeal to the African's tribal consciousness.

"What's wrong with being a German?"

"You see," said the Officer, "It is not good for one tribe to rule another. Each tribe must be for itself. Germans for Germany, French for France... it is only fair."

"Then, you British, what are you doing here?" asked the chieftain.

33)

"Is it true that in Cameroon in Africa people live up in tress?" the German journalist asked the Cameroonians student studying abroad.

"Yes," the student replied.

"How big is the three in which you live?"

"Just slightly bigger than the one in which the German ambassador lives," was the reply.

34)

Field Marshall Mobutu, the Zaire head of state was known to be extremely rich.

"Mr. President," a journalist addressed him at the airport in Paris. "You are said to be the world's third richest man. How do you feel about that?"

"It is not true," said the billionaire President.

"I am the fourth, not the third."

35)

A boy had hoped to have enough money to entertain friends for Christmas, so he sent out invitations. At the last minute he had only 50francs to use. He decided to go on with the invitation, but also hide his disappointment. He bought rice for 50francs, stewed it and threw it on the floor and scattered some round the table. He went to a nearby bar and gathered new beer corks, went to a restaurant and asked for chicken bones for his dog. Returning home he scattered the beer covers and bones all over he ran into his bed and pretended to be deep asleep.

When they succeeded in getting out of bed he told them he was suffering from the hangover of the party the previous night which they missed.

"But you said today," one guest said.

"I said yesterday," the man said. "See the remains of what we consumed.

We had to stop the car and take in the young man. He seemed to be in some kind of trouble, from the way he was running and looking behind.

"Any problem?" we asked as soon as he jumped into the car.

"No problem sa. Anything I want a ride I run like that and people stop."

37)

No taxi would take him because he looked very wet. And why was he wet? The shirt he had recently bought bore the label: WASH AND WEAR. When he noticed that the shirt was dirty that morning he washed it and immediately obeyed the second part of the instructions.

38)

A man went out hunting and when he saw a lion coming he took cover and waited until it came within firing range. He then stepped out and pulled the trigger, but he discovered that there was no cartridge in the gun. Desperate he threw the gun away and knelt down and began to pray. The lion came up to the frightened man and also knelt down before him.

"What are you doing?" he asked the lion.

"Saying my grace before meals," the lion replied.

At a police checkpoint a man was found sitting with a human skull in his hands.

"You have to be charged for that. Why are you carrying a human skull?" the policeman asked.

"Because two heads are better than one," the man said.

40)

A new bookshop put up the following advertisement:

NEW ARRIVALS: SHORT-CUTS TO EVERYTHING

1.   TENNIS IN SIX MONTHS WITHOUT A NET
2.   LEARN COOKERY IN THREE DAYS WITHOUT A FIRE
3.   SWIMMING IN ONE MONTH WITHOUT A SWIMMING POOL
4.   FRENCH IN 6 MONTHS WITHOUT OPENING YOUR LIPS.

41)

A prostitute sat on her bed in a brothel when a man knocked and entered. The woman knew what he had come for. Bu the man gave a condition:

"Before I make'am you must quench lamp.

And after every round I must go down for piss."

She said she had no problem with that, provided the price was right. The man gave her 2,000francs, she put out the light and then immediately went to work. Round one, he went to "piss" as agreed upon. Round two he went down, round three, four, five, six and at the seventh she could no longer stand it.

For one thing, each time he returned he seemed much stronger than before. A bit suspicious, the harlot put on the lights to see what kind of man she was dealing with.

But the man she saw was not the one with whom she had negotiated the original deal.

"You go pay for all tha seben people wey dem dong sleep me," the woman clung to him.

"No one day," the man said. "Go down ask the man we i de sell tickets for people for come sleep I woman for this room."

10

MACARA PARTY

1)

Probably because it was imported, but mainly because it was expensive, Becks beer was the beer of the rich in Cameroon. A man once invited people to a party in his compound, and as he went round greeting his guests he found his night watchman with two bottles of Becks under his armpit.

"Pa!" he shouted in surprise. "You drink Becks?"

"Yes, why not?" the old man asked. "I fear who?"

"You know that if you drink Becks rats will bite your lips in the night?"

"I will rub rat poison for my mouth before I sleep," the man said and opened one of the bottles.

2)

The lonely man, drinking outside the bar was concerned that some five customers had not been attended to. He went in and called the barman to come and serve the men. The bar man, not the best in the job, walked up to the group and announced:

"That man at the corner says I should give you people a drink."

And when the bill of 1000francs was made he took it to the man who had disturbed his sleep.

"So I committed a crime in asking you to serve your customers?" he asked.

3)

"How much is a bottle of beer?" the man asked the countryside barman.

"One thousand francs sa," the man said.

"For how many bottles?"

"One," the barman stressed.

"To say Jesus come here," the visitor said to himself, "he go change even dust into wine."

4)

From the distance you would think they were singing a familiar church tune. But up close all they were singing was "N-e-a-r-e-r my cup to me..."

5)

The man had been out the whole afternoon, drinking and advising his son most of the time, about the dangers of alcohol.

"But how do you know when to stop drinking?" the worried boy asked his father "Easy," the man said. "You see these fou bottles in front of us?"

The boy looked round and saw only two bottles. At any rate he answered his father.

"When they become eight, or ten, or something like that," the man went on. "Then I know it is time to stop."

6)

"Ladies and gentlemen," the Master of a certain ceremony rose and began. "The chairman of this occasion is somebody very familiar to you." He then went on to speak for thirty minutes, and when he said " now hand you over to the chairman to make his opening remarks, somebody commented?

"If the M.C. took thirty minutes to introduce the chairman, then the chairman's opening remarks will take all day!"

7)

When the town soccer team won the provincial soccer trophy, everybody went wild with drinking. So such occasions poor people take advantage of the rich and drink for free. In a certain bar a gentleman entered and asked for two bottles of beer for himself. He then called for the barman.

"Give them drinks," he said. "When I drink, everybody must drink."

The man did as he demanded. He quickly finished his beer but paid for his own share only.

"What will happen with our own drinks?" one of the people who had benefited from his generosity enquired.

"When I drink; everybody must drink," he repeated. "And when I pay everybody must pay!"

8)

"When did the police release you?" a gentleman hoping to put off his friend who was sitting with a girl asked.

"Immediately after they released you," the other said.

9)

"Where are you going to, with those bottles of gin in your pocket," the host of a party asked a cunning guest.

"Ah-ah!" the guest exclaimed. "You know that when I come home from a place like this I always like to take something for the children."

10)

"When are doing in the gutter there, Bernard?" a man asked his neighbour who lay drunk, snoring with his eyes open.

"I just went up there and took only one beer.

Then as I was passing my foot went into this gutter. Anyway no problem. The houses are passing. As soon as I see my own I will get out and go inside."

11)

"Did you not see the notice up there?" the landlord asked a man who left the bar and was urinating in front of his house.

"When notice?" the man from the bar asked as he did his own thing.

The landlord pointed to a board half-way up the wall saying:

DO NOT URINATE HERE.

"But have I urinate up the wall there?" the man asked the landlord.

12)

"Anybody has lost some money here?" the barman asked aloud after he had been talking to a customer.

Several hands shot up."

"You have found some?" somebody asked him.

"No," the barman said. "Many people keep going about saying that they lost money here. I just wanted to know whether it is true.

13)

People sat drinking in the veranda of an old wooden house when a man leaning against the wall heard a noise behind him. A piece of wood gave way and a woman's showed up under his armpit.

He grabbed it and sat drinking his beer without saying a word.

"Andrew," he heard a woman cry from within. "My leg."

"What about your leg?" Andrew asked.

"My leg is outside. My foot broke through the wall as you were pushing me, and somebody is holding it outside."

Andrew rose and looked round the bed. It was true. He put on his shirt, walked casually out to the veranda and looked into the line of people sitting against the wall until he found a man with his girlfriend's leg under his armpit.

He did not ask the man why he was holding his girlfriend's foot. He simply called the barman and told him:

"Give that man there a crate of whatever he is drinking."

The trick worked, for as soon as the drinks were brought the food fell suddenly from the man's grip. Beer works wonders!

14)

The man had been drinking for several hours, but nevertheless, it occurred to him that he recognized the woman who had greeted him and was trying in vain to make him listen to what she was saying.

"I am James Amba…" he began to introduce himself.

"I know," the woman said.

"Ho nice. What's your name?"

"Sussana," she said

"Where do you live?"

"Mbingo Street," she said.

"That's where I live too," the man said.

"Where in Mbingo Street?"

the woman described the building.

"But that's where I live too."

"Yes, we live there together," she said. "I am your wife."

The alcohol cleared from his eyes immediately.

15)

"Can you call that lady over there for me?" the gentleman at the bar asked the lady serving them.

When the lady was called he asked her to take a drink on him. That was done and while she was drinking the woman who been sent to call her came up to the gentleman and said:

"Now that I have brought you the lady, how about me? I hope you won't throw me away."

"I send a dog to catch an animal, do I then leave the animal it has caught to eat the dog?" the man asked.

16)

The little landlord walked into the bar in which a tenant a bully who owed him several months of rents was drinking and said to the barman:

"One full bottle of big whisky please."

Everybody sat quiet.

"One bottle?"

"I say one bottle."

The whisky was brought out and as soon as he paid for it he opened it and as he drank from the bottle he was telling himself loudly:

"Let anybody who is owing me in this house not pay that money at one and I will transfer all this whisky to his head."

To the consternation of the people he emptied the drink. He then went up to the debtor and asked him:

"Are you ready to pay me all money now or die?"

"I have only half," the bully said, for once, afraid of the little man.

"Give me and write a cheque for the rest."

The bully did exactly as he was told.

But later on it was discovered the landlord and the barman had played a trick on the bully. It was a bottle of tea that was handed over to him, not whisky!

17)

A male horse which a guest had ridden to a party was grazing across the road from the scene of the action when one woman, without knowing that she was being overhead whispered to the friend as the horse urinated:

"O look at how God wastes things. If instead of the needle my husband had this, what would I beg be going out for?"

18)

At the send-off party the parting friend rose and thought he should be brief, so he said: "I thank you from the bottom of my heart and from my wife's own bottom."

19)

It was the most spectacular reversal of roles ever. Regular customers to the JP Drinking Spot had complained to the proprietor that rats were always disturbing them as they sat drinking. They suggested that he should buy rattraps.

The man promised to find a permanent solution to the problem. He bought not rattraps but a kitten. Two days after arrival of the kitten the customers sat drinking one afternoon when the cat charged across the veranda into the main road.

"Yes," one customer said. "This cat really knows the job. "At last we shall drink in peace."

The assumption was that the cat was chasing a rat. Seconds later, a rat not much smaller than the cat charged out of the room, apparently looking for the cat that almost lost its life under the wheels of a passing vehicle.

20)

A boy who had given his coat to his friend to attend a dance with found him jumping all over the place. He walked up to him as he danced and whispered in his ear:

"If you are jumping like that you should know that it is a new coat. I have not even finish paying all the money."

21)

"O, this life!" cried a drunkard as he sipped his drink in a bar. "Those who have died must be regretting now about how much they have missed. Look at beer which used to cost 200francs, only 150 now."

22)

"Would you want another beer?" a Cameroonian barman asked.

"Of course," the customer said." A cold one this time. After all, Cameroon is a bilingual country."

23)

Philip knew that Nji was allergic to pepper. So when the chicken was brought in at the party they were attending he decided to put off his friend.

"What kind of pepper did you put in this chicken that it is tasting like this?" he asked the boy serving them.

24)

It was the climax of the evening's activities mealtime and the pastor was called upon to lead prayers.

"That the almighty Lord should send down his spirits to guide us and…" he began when he noticed a dog under the table, trying to take advantage of the silence to steal meat.

"Amos, send that dog away," he said.

"Amen," the people said. After all they were all-hungry and did not care how the prayer sounded.

25)

"I think I have met this face before," the man told the woman drinking by him, hoping thereby to open up a conversation. "I just that I have forgotten where."

"Perhaps," she said. "But it has always been in front of my head."

"How does one get to be served in this place?" a customer who had been waiting for a long time asked.

"Just put your finger on that red thing," (he was referring to the switch on the wall), "Press it. Somebody will come and attend to you."

The man did just that, but by some coincidence the switch developed a fault and went on ringing without stopping, even after he had removed his finger.

"I hope you did not forget your finger on the switch," the man who had directed him said. The visitor turned, looked first at the switch and then at his hand. Then he said: "No it is not there. My finger is right here with me."

27)

A young man walked to an elderly person drinking at a bar and said:

"Pa, I,…I wanted to pay for another drink for you but I did not have enough money."

"How much do you have?" the old man asked.

"I lack only twenty-five francs," the boy said.

The man searched his pocket and handed the boy twenty-five francs. After all if he could get another beer just by spending twenty-five francs, it was a good bargain. But he would waiting in vain for his drink because the boy walked away as soon as he got the money.

28)

In another similar situation, four men walked into a bar and found most of the tables occupied. There was one with four chairs, but one of them was occupied by a gentleman. One of the newcomers went up to him and said:

"Oga, finish your drink quickly and take another one."

The man who had been sipping slowly gulped down the drink and sat waiting. Instead of giving him the promised drink one of the men went up to the barman and said:

"We are four of us, and there is one man sitting behind an empty glass over there. Ask him to leave so that we can use the seats."

A fight broke out that lasted for several hours.

29)

It began to drizzle, and a man parked his car near the road. He did not bother to take out the radio-cassette, and gradually darkness overtook them in the bar. About an hour later somebody ran into the bar to tell the owner of the car that he might have locked up his child in the car.

"It must be a thief!" he shouted and they all ran out to catch him. A man had, in fact entered the car and taken out the radio-cassette with the intention of carrying it away when he discovered that he had been trapped in the car.

Thew man's car usually had radiator problems, so he carried a gallon of water in the trunk.

"I am going to burn this car," he shouted to the hearing of the thief inside, and immediately went to the trunk and took out the gallon of water which looked like a gallon of fuel and began sprinkling all over the car.

"This car is insured against fire and theft," he said, and struck a match. The man inside passed out instantly.

30)

"Cut you goat according to your size" the Chief announced at a garden party.

31)

When asked the meaning of RSVP., a character in Chinua Achebe's novel No Longer At Ease, said: "It means Rice and Stew Very Plentiful."

"Or that is how your face is?" the man enquired impudently.

"Opening please," the man said to the barman. "You know it is a bit hard to drink without opening the bottle."

A blackman entered a bar in South Africa and took his seat at a corner. The white waiter walked up to him and said:

"Excuse me sir, we don't serve blacks here."

"I didn't say you should should serve me blacks," the man said. "I want only a chicken."

When he insisted and was served, he had barely taken up his cutlery when three husky white boys came in and marched up to him.

"If you dare do anything to that chicken we shall do exactly that to you," one of the bullies warned. The blackman, on hearing this picked up the chicken and kissed it.

35)

"What are you called?" the man asked the lady customer who came in and sat opposite his table. Thinking that the man had asked her what she wanted to eat, she said:

"Spagheti."

"O, very nice name," the man said, having never heard of the meal before.

36)

The chiefs had been invited and had been told to bring along only one wife each. Three chiefs passed, then three woman, and then as a fourth woman tried to enter, the gate man asked:

"You are who?"

"The second chief's wife," she said, meaning that she was the wife of the chief who went in second.

"No way to way," the gate man said. "One chief one wife. Na so them talk."

11

CHORSE

1)

"Even to go to heaven," said the Pastor as he tried to sooth emotions at a funeral, you have to die first. Our brother has just taken the first step towards heaven."

2)

"What is the Acts of the Apostles?" the Pastor asked.

"The Axe which the Good Samaritan used to cut the robber trees that fell on the traveller," came the reply.

3)

"I notice with deepest disappointment," began the Pastor after a prayer session, "That some five or six faithfuls did not close their eyes at all, and that two people at the back closed only one eye.

That," he ended up," is a sign of impiety to the Almighty."

4)

"What did Christ mean when he said "no man can serve two masters?" asked the village catechist.

"He meant that no man should marry two wives," said a much-maligned husband.

5)

"You must choose a new name, a Christian name," the missionary said to the woman. She would not.

"Why?" he asked her.

"My man will not know me again when we meet in the next world."

6)

"I stole a rope," the avid Christian said to the priest at confession.

The priest nodded and gave him his penance. "Two Our Fathers three times a day for one week. Go."

He noticed that the man was still kneeling by the window on the other wide.

"Anything else?" the priest asked.

"Yes, father."

"What?"

"There was a goat tied to the rope that I stole."

"Idiot!" shouted the priest. "Say you stole a goat, not a rope. Hell is waiting for people like you."

7)

A newly ordained pastor showed up for the first time in his village church.

"I will take for my text today," he began,

"The feeding of the multitude: and they fed five men with five thousand fishes," he said nervously. At this misquotation, an old parishioner said audibly:

"That's no miracle. I could do it myself."

The young pastor was silent.

The following Sunday he announced the same text, but this time he got it right:

"And they fed five thousand people with five loaves of bread."

He waited a moment and leaning over the pulpit and looking at the old man asked:

"And could you do that too?"

"Of course," the man said.

"How?" the embarrassed pastor enquired.

"With what was left over last Sunday," he said.

8)

"And the whale swallowed Jonas," a pastor said in the course of his sermon.

There was a long laugh. Confused, he thought he had made a mistake, and then tried to correct himself.

"And Jonas swallowed the whale," he said nervously. There was an even louder laugh. He was now desperate. Unable to know what to do he declared: "whether Jonas swallowed the whale or the whale swallowed Jonas, what I know is that there was some swallowing."

9)

A young woman called Martha took her pagan husband to church for the first time. The attendance was poor and, and the preacher could not hide his feelings.

"What's the matter with members of this church?" he wondered aloud; "They seem to abandon God every week. Let somebody really tell me what the matter is."

As they left the Church to return home the husband was silent for a very long time.

"What is happening?" Martha tried to open a conversation with him.

"You will tell me what you and that preacher have that he should call only your name in front of me like that," the angry man said.

10)

The telephone to heaven rang.

"St. Peter speaking," the voice answered at the reception.

"Blessed Saint," the caller began, "Is it true that there will be a last judgement?"

"Absolutely," said the holy one.

"How will that be?" the caller enquired.

"The bones shall rise again and each shall be tried according to his sins," St. Peter explained.

"Where will that be?"

"In the judgement hall."

"You mean Ojuku's bones will rise with Gowon's bones together?"

"You bet."

"That Hitler and the Jews will be together?"

"I don't see why not."

"That Anglophones and Francophones will be together?"

"Certainly," St. Peter said.

"That my father and my mother shall sit together again?"

"Yes, holy one. Are there any policemen in heaven?"

"No. Why?"

"Because only a policeman will keep these people that I have mentioned from fighting again."

11)

A Reverend father was visiting a girl at the same time that a student was with her. As soon as the student heard the man's voice he ran up the barn and hid there. The unscrupulous girl obliged the father's lascivious desires. Midway through the exercise she asked:

"But father, what will happen if I get pregnant?"

"Never mind. That guy up there will take care of you," he said pointing to the ceiling, but actually referring to God.

"Let nobody involve me in your affairs," the boy cried from the barn, thinking that the Reverend was about to transfer his responsibilities to him.

11.a)

Another version has it that the priest was making love to the girl under a palm tree in which a taper was resting. When the girl expressed her fears and the priest pointed up, the taper shouted:

"God go punish woman for there. You go sleep woman me I care for pikin nobi so?"

12)

Another priest was trapped in a woman's hut in the village. He climbed up the barn and hid, hoping that the woman's husband would spend only a short time with her and go out. The man instead took off his clothes and sat in his lounge chair. The Reverend Father was expected to lead Benediction in church later that evening, so he had to return to his parish. An idea came to his mind. He jumped from the barn on to the floor, shouting:

"I come from up to bring blessings to this house," and walked away, rosary in hand.

13)

An even more licentious priest drove from a brothel straight to church with what he thought was his white handkerchief in the pocket of his cassock. At a certain stage in his delivery of the gospel he wanted to emphasis the whiteness of the soul.

"Even this handkerchief is not white enough for the state of the soul when you enter heaven."

So saying he pulled out and held to the congregation's shocked view a lady's underpants.

14)

Two neighbours had quarrelled and sworn and insulted God over a piece of land. The following day was Sunday, and as one stood in front of the church he saw the other coming. As the man tried to enter the church the man stepped in front of him and said:

"You mean you will insult God like that and then just come to church without going for confession?"

15)

It was a law with the church that nobody who had willingly sinned should go for communication until he had first gone for confession.

The night before a man had left his wife at home to go and meet his girlfriend. But he said he was attending an official meeting. The following day the woman was surprised to notice that her husband did not rise to go for communion in church. On his part the man was surprised that she too did not rise. After mass he went straight to he and asked:

"Tell me the truth, why did you not go for communion?"

"Tell me the truth too," she said. "why did you not go for communion?"*

16)

The mission TV set was stolen along with the video cassette deck. The police was called in, but to no avail. Then one day the parish priest was listening to confessions from behind his closet when a man said:

"I have come to ask father to ask God to forgive me."

"What did you do?" the priest asked calmly. "The almighty is always forgiving."

"I was the one who store the mission TV."

"And what about the deck?" the priest asked, lowering his head to see the criminal through the small opening on the wall."

"I stole that too," he admitted.

"Where are the things now?"

"I sold them yesterday, father."

"This is not a case for the almighty," the priest shouted; "It is a police case; You cannot steal mission property and expect church penance."

17)

A woman once wore her twenty-five year old wedding garment, complete with veil to church. She was an instant centre of attraction.

"Where is your partner?' the embarrassed priest asked when she showed up for communion.

"He is sick in the village," she replied.

"Then why do you come wearing this?" the priest asked.

"When he was going to the village he told me that he will wear the suit he wore on the day of our marriage to church today."

18)

It was only the third meeting of the Christian Women's Fellowship. But already the president was sensing trouble.

"There are some women in here," she began in a severe tone," they want to try me. Anything I wear they sew the same thing; Let that stop. If you came here only to imitate people, you should return to your houses."

19)

"Alelujah," the pastor cried
"Place de hot," an old man answered.

20)

The villagers seemed to have taken too much of alcohol. This the new priest meant to stamp out. The very next Sunday he showed up in church with a glass of alcohol. At the appropriate moment he produced the glass and in a bid to show them the precise dangers of alcohol he pulled out a live earthworm from a jar and put into the alcohol. It died instantly.

"So it also kills worms!" one of the onlookers exclaimed.

THE END

12

FOR *MOOMOOS* ONLY NOTHING INSIDE, BUT P.T.O.

Moomoo is another name for a fool!

The instructions were clear: first of all you were told that you had come to the end. You seemed not to have taken that seriously. You were next told that the rest of the material belonged to *moomoos*, but that you could, how ever, turn over the page.

The choice was then yours, to prove that you were not a *moomoo*, by shutting the book and going you away, or, confirming that you are indeed *a moomoo* by turning over the page.

P.T.O.

So now, as I was saying the other time, if anybody calls you a fool, will you blame him? Answer that question as honestly as you possibly can, knowing that many of us out here already know the answer.

THE END, WHETHER YOU LIKE IT OR NOT

Titles by *Langaa RPCIG*

Ignasio Malizani Jimu
Urban Appropriation and Transformation: Bicycle Taxi
and Handcart Operators

Joyce B. Ashuntantang
Landscaping and Coloniality: The Dissemination of
Cameroon Anglophone Literature
A Basket of Flaming Ashes

Jude Fokwang
Mediating Legitimacy: Chieftaincy and Democratisation in
Two African Chiefdoms

Michael A. Yanou
Dispossession and Access to Land in South Africa:
an African Perspective

Tikum Mbah Azonga
Cup Man and Other Stories
The Wooden Bicycle and Other Stories

John Nkemngong Nkengasong
Letters to Marions (And the Coming Generations)
The Call of Blood

Amady Aly Dieng
Les étudiants africains et la littérature négro-africaine
d'expression française

Tah Asongwed
Born to Rule: Autobiography of a life President
Child of Earth

Frida Menkan Mbunda
Shadows From The Abyss

Bongasu Tanla Kishani
A Basket of Kola Nuts
Konglanjo (Spears of Love without Ill-fortune) and
Letters to Ethiopia with some Random Poems

Fo Angwafo III S.A.N of Mankon
Royalty and Politics: The Story of My Life

Basil Diki
The Lord of Anomy
Shrouded Blessings

Churchill Ewumbue-Monono
Youth and Nation-Building in Cameroon: A Study of
National Youth Day Messages and Leadership Discourse
(1949-2009)

**Emmanuel N. Chia, Joseph C. Suh & Alexandre
Ndeffo Tene**
Perspectives on Translation and Interpretation in
Cameroon

Linus T. Asong
The Crown of Thorns
No Way to Die
A Legend of the Dead: Sequel of The Crown of Thorns
The Akroma File
Salvation Colony: Sequel to No Way to Die
Chopchair
Doctor Frederick Ngenito
The Crabs of Bangui
Laughing Store: A Treasury of Entertainment

Vivian Sihshu Yenika
Imitation Whiteman
Press Lake Varsity Girls: The Freshman Year

Beatrice Fri Bime
Someplace, Somewhere
Mystique: A Collection of Lake Myths

Shadrach A. Ambanasom
Son of the Native Soil
The Cameroonian Novel of English Expression:
An Introduction

Education of the Deprived: Anglophone Cameroon
Literary Drama
Homage and Courtship (Romantic Stirrings of a Young Man)

**Tangie Nsoh Fonchingong and Gemandze John
Bobuin**
Cameroon: The Stakes and Challenges of Governance and
Development

Tatah Mentan
Democratizing or Reconfiguring Predatory Autocracy?
Myths and Realities in Africa Today
Roselyne M. Jua & Bate Besong
To the Budding Creative Writer: A Handbook

Albert Mukong
Prisoner without a Crime: Disciplining Dissent in
Ahidjo's Cameroon

Mbuh Tennu Mbuh
In the Shadow of my Country

Bernard Nsokika Fonlon
Genuine Intellectuals: Academic and Social
Responsibilities of Universities in Africa
Challenge of Culture in Africa: From Restoration to
Integration

Lilian Lem Atanga
Gender, Discourse and Power in the Cameroonian
Parliament

Cornelius Mbifung Lambi & Emmanuel Neba Ndenecho
Ecology and Natural Resource Development
in the Western Highlands of Cameroon: Issues in Natural
Resource Managment

Gideon F. For-mukwai
Facing Adversity with Audacity

Peter W. Vakunta & Bill F. Ndi
Nul n'a le monopole du français : deux poètes du
Cameroon anglophone

Emmanuel Matateyou
Les murmures de l'harmattan

Ekpe Inyang
The Hill Barbers

JK Bannavti
Rock of God (Kilán ke Nyúy)

Godfrey B. Tangwa (Rotcod Gobata)
I Spit on their Graves: Testimony Relevant to the
Democratization Struggle in Cameroon
Road Companion to Democracy and Meritocracy (Further
Essays from an African Perspective)

Henrietta Mambo Nyamnjoh
"We Get Nothing from Fishishing", Fishing for Boat
Opportunies amongst Senegalese Fisher Migrants

Bill F. Ndi, Dieurat Clervoyant & Peter W. Vakunta
Les douleurs de la plume noire : du Cameroun
anglophone à Haïti

Laurence Juma
Kileleshwa: A Tale of Love, Betrayal and Corruption in
Kenya

Nol Alembong
Forest Echoes (Poems)

Marie-Hélène Mottin-Sylla & Joëlle Palmieri
Excision : les jeunes changent l'Afrique par les TIC

Walter Gam Nkwi
Voicing the Voiceless: Contributions to Closing Gaps in
Cameroon History, 1958-2009

John Koyela Fokwang
A Dictionary of Popular Bali Names

Alain-Joseph Sissao
(Translated from the French by Nina Tanti)
Folktales from the Moose of Burkina Faso

Colin Ayeab Diyen
The Earth in Peril

E. M. Chilver
Zintgraff's Explorations in Bamenda, Adamawa and
the Benue Lands 1889—1892

Célestine Colette Fouellefak Kana
Valeurs religieuses et développement durable : une
approche d'analyse des institutions des Bamiléké du
Cameroun

Piet Konings
Crisis and Neoliberal Reforms in Africa: Civil Society and
Agro-Industry in Anglophone Cameroon's Plantation
Economy

Christopher Chi Che
Aspect of History, Language, Culture, Flora and Fauna

Peter Acho Awoh
The Dynamics and Contradictions of Evangelisation in
Africa: An Essay on the Kom Christian Experience